UNDERSTANDING PHOTOTYPESETTING

UNDERSTANDING PHOTO TYPESETTING

Written and illustrated by
Michael L. Kleper

Assistant Professor of Graphic Arts
Rochester Institute of Technology

North American Publishing Company • Philadelphia

This book is dedicated to
the memory of my father
who, besides all his other achievements
and wonders, encouraged my interest in type
and who presented me with my first Kelsey press
more than fifteen years ago.

Copyright © 1976 by North American Publishing Company

All rights reserved. Except for brief quotations
in critical reviews, no part of this book may be reproduced
or utilized in any form or by any means,
electronic or mechanical, including photocopying, recording
or by an information storage and retrieval system,
without permission in writing from the Publisher.
Inquiries should be addressed to
North American Publishing Company,
401 North Broad Street, Philadelphia, Pennsylvania 19108.

Library of Congress Catalog Number: 75-27942
ISBN: 0-912920-46-7
Order number: 138

Printed in the United States of America

To the Reader

This book is designed with you in mind.
Each chapter builds upon the preceding one
in what is considered a logical production order.
Also, each chapter has a summary at the beginning
(rather than at the end) to provide both
an introduction to new and unfamiliar material,
and also to serve as a refresher
in subsequent references to the chapter.
The summary is followed by a listing
of technical terms which is placed
before the specific text it explains,
rather than at the end of the book,
to make it more readily available for referral.

Acknowledgements

I wish to thank my wife, Gwen,
for reading and correcting the manuscript
and understanding the hundreds of hours
needed for "the project";
Jodi, for understanding why Daddy was too tired
to get up for the two o'clock feeding;
Bob and Barbara Tompkins for reading
and correcting the manuscript,
and for making some good suggestions.

CONTENTS

1 typography

Summary 1
Trade Terms 2
Introduction 5
Metal Type 6
Typographic Measurement 8
Metric Type Sizes 9
The Keyboard Layout 10
The Use of Space 10
    Justification 11
    Quadding 11
    Ragged Right 11
    Indention 11
    Letterspacing 11
    Kerning 11
    Wordspacing 12
    Leading 12
    Line Length 13
Physical Elements of Type
    Design 13
Single Face Variations 15
Typeface Geometry 17
Type Classification 18
The Parts of a Page 19
Legibility and Readability 20

2 photolettering machines

Summary 21
Trade Terms 22
Introduction 23
History 23
Photolettering Techniques 25
The Blind Machines 28
Visual Machines 34

	The Keyboard Machines............... 39
	Other Cold Type Methods............. 41

3 direct impression typesetting

Summary............................. 46
Trade Terms.......................... 47
Introduction.......................... 48
Composition Components on
    Direct Impression Surfaces........... 49
Proportional Versus Fixed
    Spacing.......................... 52
Justification.......................... 54
Advantage of Direct Impression
    Typesetting....................... 56
The AM VariTyper, the IBM
    Composer and Others............... 57

4 input devices

Summary............................. 58
Trade Terms.......................... 59
Introduction.......................... 61
Keyboards............................ 61
    Keyboard Classification.............. 63
    Keyboard Options................... 66
    Keyboard Output.................... 67
    The Coding System.................. 67
    Precedence Codes................... 68
    Reading Paper Tape................. 69
    Magnetic Tape...................... 71
    Other Recording Media.............. 71
    Word Processing.................... 73
    Keyboard Layout.................... 73
    Direct Keyboarding.................. 74
Mark-up.............................. 76

5 editing devices

Summary 84
Trade Terms 85
Introduction 85
Error Detection and
    Elimination 86
    Author's Alterations 87
    Corrections 88
    Blind, non-counting
       Keyboards 88
    Use of a Computer 88
    The VDT 89
    Use of a VDT 91
    CAM 95
Matrix Proofers 96
VDT Manufacturers 98

6 phototypesetting machines

Summary 100
Trade Terms 101
Introduction 102
The Basic Components 102
    Image Masters 105
Point Size 109
The First Generation 110
The Development of the
    Second Generation Machine 112
The Third Generation 112
Machine Capabilities 115
H and J 116
Speed 117
Advantages and Disadvantages
    of Phototypesetting 118
Manufacturers 119

7 phototypesetting as a system

Summary 122
Trade Terms 123
Introduction 123
System Components 124
The Computer as a System 131
The Printing System 135

8 processing methods and materials

Summary 139
Trade Terms 140
Introduction 141
The Construction of Light-
    Sensitive Materials 141
    Exposure and Processing 142
Stabilization Processing 143
Other Light-Sensitive Materials 144
Automatic Precessors 144

9 paste-up methods and materials

Summary 147
Trade Terms 148
Introduction 148
The Layout 149
    Workmarks 149
Paper Paste-up 151
    Paste-up Tools 151
    Adhesives 154
Positive Film Make-up 155

Bibliography 156
Index 160

1 typography

Summary

Typography deals with the selection, arrangement, and use of type. Many methods and terms related to typography today are based on the original process of using *metal* type.

Type is measured in *points*, and there are 72 points to the inch. Lines of type and page dimensions are measured in *picas*. There are 6 picas to the inch, 12 points to the pica. The square of the point size is called the *em*. The em is a unit of space and is divided into two to five parts to form other spacing units. Columns of advertising matter are measured in *agate lines*. There are 14 agate lines to the inch.

The collection of all of the typographic characters of a particular typeface and size is called a *font*. Various kinds of typesetting, such as that for newspapers, book printing, and specialty magazines, require different font arrangements (kinds of characters) or *layouts*. These differences can be seen in the keyboard layouts of input devices for phototypesetting machines.

There are many variations of a single typeface (italic, boldface, small caps, etc.) which typographers can use for various elements of a layout. The relationships of size, weight, line, and space, are all important.

Lines of type of equal length are called *justified* lines. Lines set flush with the left margin are *quad left*, lines flush to the right are *quad right*. Centers lines are *quad center*.

Space added between letters is called *letterspacing*. The opposite is kerning or reducing space between letters. *Wordspacing* is adding or reducing space between words. The space between lines of type is called *leading*.

Typefaces are sometimes classified according to the presence or absence of a *serif*. Categories of designs are based upon physical characteristics of typefaces.

Trade Terms

agate line - a measurement of the column depth of advertising space. There are fourteen agate lines to the inch.

apex - the uppermost part of certain typographic characters where two stems meet.

arm - that part of certain typographic characters which projects horizontally or slopes upward.

ascender - referring either to that part of a lower case letter which projects upward, above the body of the letter, or to the actual letter itself (b, d, f, h, or l.)

bar - that part of certain typographic characters which is an enclosed horizontal stroke.

base line - an imaginary line upon which all capital and most lower case (except descenders) letters align.

bold face - type which is relatively darker or heavier in appearance than other type near which it is set.

cap line - one of four typographic lines of reference. The uppermost limit of capitals and ascenders.

characters - typographic units such as letters, figures, and punctuation.

character count (c.c.) - either a predetermined measurement of the approximate number of characters of a specific type size and design which can be set in one linear pica, or the actual count of each character and space in a piece of copy.

composition - the process of setting type.

copyfitting - determining the space needed to fit typeset matter.

cross stroke - that part of a typographic character which cuts across the stem.

cursive - a type design which appears flowing, like handwriting, but its letters are unconnected.

descender - that portion of a lower case letter which falls below the base line.

display type - type sizes larger than 14-point used for headlines or to otherwise attract attention.

ear - the projection found on certain lower case "g's."

em - square of the type size.

en - one half the width of the em.

font - the collection of all letters, numbers, and punctuation of a particular size of a typeface.

foundry type - metal type made in a foundry. Sold by the font.

hand composition - setting type manually.

headline - a display line at the top of a page.

hot metal - any typesetting process involving molten lead.

italic - a forward slanting variation of an upright or roman type design.

justification - the addition or subtraction of space from between words or letters to cause a line of type to exactly fit a measure.

kerning - the closer than normal fitting of letters to achieve a more pleasing appearance.

keyboard - an input device which is used to cause typographic characters to be composed in the order in which the keys are struck.

keyboard layout - the arrangement of keys to suit a particular purpose.

layout - a drawing or representation of what a finished printed job will look like.

leading (led'ing) - basically refers to the white space which appears between lines of type. In phototypesetting this space is achieved by advancing the photographic material and is, therefore, commonly called "line" or "film advance."

legibility - how well the letters of the alphabet can be understood.

letterspacing - inserting space between letters to justify a line, or improve appearance.

Linotype - a hot-metal typesetting machine which produces solid lines of type called "slugs." Corrections to such composition are made by merely replacing the slugs which contain errors.

magazine - that part of a Linotype machine which holds the matrices (molds) which are assembled to form lines and into which hot lead is forced to make slugs. A different magazine is required for each typeface and point size.

mean line - one of the typographic lines of reference. Uppermost limit of the main part of most lower case letters.

measure - the length of a full line of type measured in picas.

mixing - setting different typefaces in the same line.

Monotype - a hot-metal typesetting machine which casts individual pieces of type in composed lines. The copy is first keyboarded to produce a perforated paper tape or ribbon. The tape is run through a caster which produces the individual characters in justified form.

orphan - the last line of a page starting with an indented paragraph.

pica - measurement used to express line length. 6 picas = 1 inch.

phototypesetting - the setting of type by the exposure of light to photographic paper or film.

point - unit of measurement used to express type size. 72 points = 1 inch. 12 points = 1 pica.

point size - (type size) the measurement in points from an ascender to a descender.

proofreader's marks - internationally recognized and accepted symbols used to indicate errors and changes on proofs.

quad - a hand composition spacing material two (2-em-quad) or three (3-em-quad) times wider than the em.

quadding - positioning lines in relation to the right and left hand margins.

ragged right - lines of text which are flush against the left hand margin but end at various points on the right margin.

readability - the ease by which type can be read.

relative unit (RU) - a measure of the width of a character.

Roman - an upright letterform (in comparison to an *italic*) or a typeface based on fifteenth century humanist manuscripts.

sans serif (without serif) - a type design which does not have fine cross strokes (serifs) at the arms, stems, and tails of characters.

serif - an ending stroke drawn on the arms, tails, and stems of certain type designs.

set solid - type which is set without any leading additional to that which is designed into the typeface itself.

set width - the width of a typographic character.

slug - the product of a Linotype. A solid metal, relief, type-high line of type.

small caps - capital letters which measure as high as the lower case characters of the font.

subhead - subordinate headlines used to mark divisions in a chapter.

stem - the main part of a typographic character.

text - type sizes between 8 and 14 points.

type size - the measurement of type in points, in which one point is equal to 1/72 inch.

typographer - a person concerned with the selection, arrangement, and use of type.

typography - the process of selecting, arranging, and using type.

vertex - the lowermost part of certain typographic characters where the stems join.

widow - a single line of a length less than the measure, beginning the top of a page. Considered poor typographic style.

wordspacing - the process of adding or removing space between words to justify lines of type.

x-height - the height of the main part of lower case letters, such as "x", exclusive of ascenders and descenders.

Introduction

Typography is the process of selecting typefaces, sizes, and spacing requirements for the layout of a printed page. The actual setting of type is called composition.

The assembling of typographic characters may be accomplished by either manual or mechanical means. The most common method of setting type today is by the photographic method, thus the name phototypesetting. Despite the popularity and acceptance of phototypesetting, it is a relatively recent development, having become commercially available only within the last 20 years.

The principles of typography which are basic to phototypesetting, as well as to every other method of setting type, are carry-overs from a previous technology—the casting of type in metal. This metal composition, or hot metal typesetting, is exemplified by two major processes: the Linotype, and the Monotype. (See Figure 1.) Both machines were invented late in the nineteenth century to mechanize the slow and laborious process of hand composition. The Linotype casts lines of type called slugs from assembled lines of individual letter molds (matrices) into which molten lead is forced. The matrices are then distributed back to their proper compartment (channel) in a supply tray called a magazine.

The Monotype casts individual pieces of type in composed lines. Two machines are used: a keyboard perforator and a caster. A paper ribbon is prepared at the keyboard with precise information concerning the job to be composed. The ribbon is then fed to the casting unit where rods controlled by the perforations position character matrices over a mold, through which hot lead is pumped.

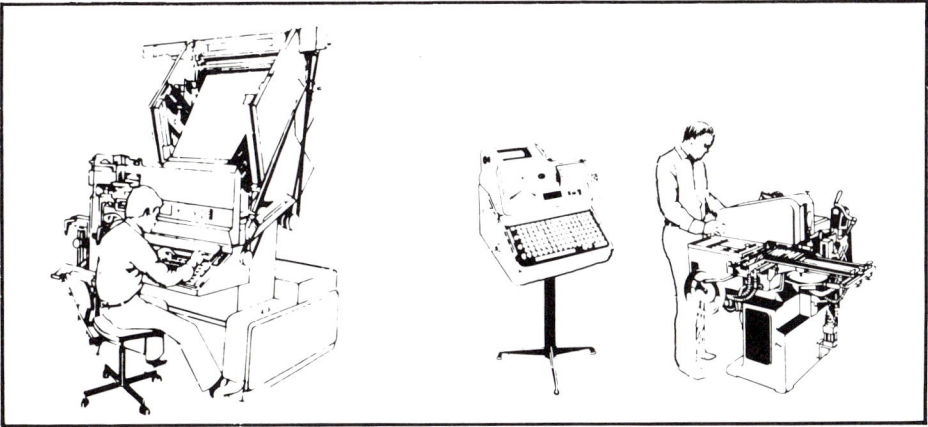

Figure 1. The Linotype machine (on the left) casts solid lines of type called "slugs" while the Monotype caster (extreme right) casts individual pieces of type as indicated through perforations on a paper tape which is punched at the keyboard. Courtesy International Paper Company

Metal Type

The earliest metal type was cast by Johann Gutenberg in the fifteenth century. Prior to that time entire book pages had been carved in wood, a very slow and exacting craft that left no margin for error. Gutenberg's invention of a hand-held mold made the mass production of type a reality. Not only could pages of type be assembled quicker, but the type could be used again and again.

Single character metal type today, either Monotype or type cast in a foundry (foundry type), bears a close resemblance to that made by Gutenberg. It is in reference to metal type that almost all typographic terminology is derived.

In Figure 2, the point size of the type is determined by the height of the type body (A). Since the typeface design is limited to the physical dimensions of the type surface, the point size of type appearing in print may be found by measuring from the uppermost reaching letters (ascenders) such as b,d,f,h,l, and t, to the lowermost reaching letters (descenders) such as g,j,p,q, and y as shown in Figure 3.

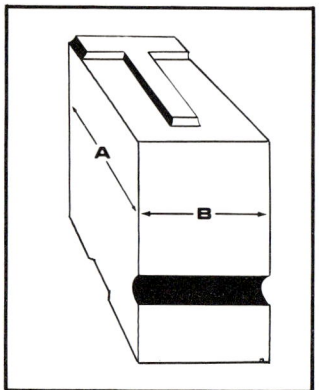

Figure 2. A piece of metal type.

Figure 3. Type is usually measured from the top of an ascender to the bottom of a descender.

It is characteristic of type that each letter be allotted a proportional width. For example, an *m* should be wider than an *i*, an *h*, wider than an *l*. In terms of metal type this measurement is called set width and is shown in Figure 2 as "B".

Typography

Set width is an important concept to typographers and typesetters since typographic characters are their building blocks and the proper fitting of letters is their business.

The set of an alphabet is based on the em. The em simply stated is the square of the point size. For example:

A 10-point em measures 10 pt. x 10 pt.
A 12-point em measures 12 pt. x 12 pt.
A 14-point em measures 14 pt. x 14 pt.

For each alphabet the em is divided into a number of parts called relative units (RU). There are commonly 18 relative units; the widest character in the font, the *M* or *W* would measure 18 units, a character half as wide such as an *e* or *z* would measure 9 units. Table 1 shows an example of the relative units of an alphabet.

Table 1. Character widths of Compugraphic font No. 0020, Futura Demibold (54-unit system).

RELATIVE UNITS	CHARACTERS
54	⅔, ⅓, %, ¾, ¼, −, ©, ®, +, ÷, ¶, =
48	W
45	m, M
42	w, O, G, Q
39	N, A
36	H, V, D, X, U
33	C, Y, K, &
30	*, o, h, n, g, p, e, d, b, x, a, u, q, k, R, P, Z, B, 1, 2, 3, 4, 5, 6, 7, 8, 9, 0, $, †, ‡, ?, #, §
27	v, f, T, E, S, F, I, •, !, -, y
24	c, z, s, L, J, /
21	r,), [, (
18	t, f, ;, :
15	l, i, j, I, ., ,, -
12	', '

Typographic Measurement

Type size is measured in points (pts.). There are 72 points to the inch, each point equal to 0.0138". Type sizes in the 9- to 12-point size range are usually used for reading matter, and are classified as text sizes. Type sizes 14 points and larger are usually used for headlines (heads) and sub-headlines (subheads), and are classified as display sizes.

```
ABCabc 8 point
ABCabc 10 point
ABCabc 12 point
ABCabc 14 point
ABCabc 18 point
ABCabc 24 point
```

Figure 4. Type sizes are measured in points.

Page dimensions and line lengths are measured in picas (pi). There are 6 picas in one inch, and 12 points in one pica. The length of a line of type is called the measure. The measure is sometimes indicated by an "X" as in X24, meaning a line length of 24 picas.

Another useful measurement is the character count (c.c.). The character count is used in copyfitting to determine how much space will be necessary to fit typeset matter. The character count is an approximation of the number of characters of a specific typeface that may be set in one linear pica. For example, the typeface Granjon, in 12-point, has a c.c. of 2.45. This means that approximately 2.45 characters of Granjon can be set in one linear pica. A line length of 18 picas would mean that (18 pi x 2.45 char./pi.) 44 characters could be set in one line. If there are 30 18-pica lines per page (30 lines x 44 char./line) then there is sufficient space for 1320 characters per page. If the typewritten manuscript (copy) contains approximately 165,000 characters, then (165,000 char.÷1320 char./page) 125 pages will be required to copyfit the manuscript.

When type is set in metal, either by machine or by hand, the space separating letters, words and lines must also be set. The system of spaces used is based on the em: the square of the point size.

Typography

Two other commonly used spacing materials are the brass thin space which measures one point, and the copper thin space which measures one-half point.

Column Dimensions

A measurement which is unique to newspapers and magazines is the agate line. It is used in measuring the depth of columns of advertising space. There are fourteen agate lines in one column-inch.

Metric Type Sizes

The flexibility of phototypesetting has lead some people to believe that a metric standard of measurement might make better use of the potential of a phototypesetting machine. One such person is S. J. Heden of Sweden, who has developed a metric system for measuring typefaces primary dimension— the mainstroke of the letter. The mainstroke of the letter is usually the same measurement as the height of the capital, and in the Heden system this is equivalent to the point size.

The basic unit of the metric system is the meter. The meter is divided in 10 parts to make 10 decimenters (dm), in 100 parts to make 100 centimeters (cm), and in 1000 parts to make 1000 millimeters (mm). Heden found that even the smallest metric unit, the millimeter, was too large for accurate typographic measurements, so he divided the millimeter into 10 parts. Each one-tenth millimeter is called a "*d*".

Figure 5. Letters are measured in terms of the "d" measurements.

Figure 6. The complete metric description of a typeface is given as a/b, the primary dimension over the secondary dimension.

The *d* value may be converted to points by multiplying by 0.4. Therefore, a typeface mainstroke measuring 90*d* would convert to a point size of 36 points (0.4 x 90*d*).

Heden also specifies a secondary dimension (see Figure 5.), which allows for the downward projection of the descenders. This secondary dimension, or mainstroke, is usually given in relation to the secondary dimension, such as 75/90, read as "75 on 90." (See Figure 6.)

The Keyboard Layout

Typesetting was originally a manual process. Typesetting by hand required that each character be located in a typecase, lifted from its compartment and placed in a composing stick (a hand-held tray). Character by character words and lines were assembled. When Linotype and Monotype machines were introduced, the process of locating characters was simplified by the touching of a key as in typewriting. The keyboard remains one of the fastest ways to set type.°

Different keyboards have various numbers of keys and various arrangements. The arrangement of keys is called the keyboard layout. The keyboard layout of a Linotype is different from a Monotype, and both are different from any modern phototypesetting keyboard. Today, most keyboards are arranged like a standard office typewriter. If a person can type he can become familiar with any modern keyboard quite easily.

Keyboards are usually arranged according to their production use. For example, newspapers print stock market reports, so they require fractions. Bookprinters need mathematical signs and footnote indicators for textbooks and other publications. Trade typographers, whose business it is to sell the output of a phototypesetting machine, require a variety of special characters.

Today, because of the large number of manufacturers of phototypesetting machines and keyboards, it is quite possible to see a keyboard and phototypesetting machine of two different manufacturers being used together. In such a case it is very important that the operator know exactly what character the phototypesetter will flash in correspondence to each keystroke.

The Use of Space

Typographers are very much concerned with the way that letters, words and lines are positioned on a page. This involves careful consideration of the white space surrounding the typeface.

°*One of the fastest methods of inputting to a phototypesetter is by Optical Character Recognition (OCR). OCR machines can electronically "read" pages of manuscript and directly operate a typesetting machine.*

Typography

Justification

Newspaper columns, and book pages usually have justified lines of type. Justification is the process of varying the space between words (wordspacing) and the space between letters (letterspacing) to make each line of type completely fill the line measure of a given block of type.

Quadding

The last line of a paragraph usually does not fill the measure. In hand composition large metal spaces two or three times as wide as an em were used to fill the space to the right of the final line. These spaces were called quads, and the process of using them was called quadding. In typeset output from a phototypesetting machine, space is simply the absence of an exposure of light to photographic paper. Quadding becomes a machine command on the positioning of less than a full line of type. The last line of a paragraph is pushed to the left, therefore quad left (ql). A line pushed to the right is quad right (qr). Centered lines are quad center (qc).

Ragged Right

If all lines on a page or in a column are quadded left, the style is called ragged right, or flush left, ragged right. The copy you are reading is set ragged right.

Indention

Just as paragraphs must end with a quad left line, they must begin with an indention. An indention is a space which sets the paragraph apart from other lines of type. Line measures of 18 picas or less are generally indented 1-1/2 ems. And measures 24 to 30 picas are indented 2 ems. Editorial style, however, sometimes dictates otherwise.

Letterspacing

The smallest spaces which printers use are the spaces between letters. In hand composition, they were the brass and copper spaces, 5-em spaces, and sometimes slivers of paper. In phototypesetting, letterspacing (letter justification), is specified as either *fixed space*, such as adding 1/2 point of space between letters, or as *variable space*, adding *x* relative units of the point size.

Kerning

The opposite of letterspacing is kerning. Instead of adding space between letters to space them out to fill a line, space is subtracted between letters. Kerning is usually done to display sizes to make letters fit better, and therefore appear more pleasing. In phototypesetting systems, space is sometimes

taken from between letters to achieve a tighter fitting line. This is sometimes called *character compensation*.

> Suddenly the door opened, and
>
> Suddenly the door opened, and
>
> Suddenly the door opened, and
>
> Suddenly the door opened, and

Wordspacing

Adjusting space between words, or wordspacing, is the point at which justification usually takes place. Wordspacing may be as wide as a 3-em space, or preferably narrower to allow the eye to scan more words and therefore read faster.

> There is no evidence of intelligent
>
> There is no evidence of intelligent
>
> There is no evidence of intelligen
>
> There is no evidence of intellige

Leading

In hand composition, pieces of type are assembled in a hand-held tray called a *composing stick*. After lines of type are spaced out or in to fit snugly in the measure, a thin (2-point) strip of lead is inserted to separate the lines. These strips are called *leads,* and the space between lines of type is called leading. If no leads are inserted, the lines are said to be *set solid.* Leading is customarily 20% of the point size. For example, the leading for a 10-point type would be (20% of 10 points) 2 points. It would be noted as 10/12, read as "10 on 12," the 10 being the point size, and the 12 being the point size body and the leading together. In phototypesetting systems, leading is called *line spacing* or *film advance* and is usually measured from base line to base line.

10/10	10/11
qxl qxl qxl qxl qxl qxl qxl qxl qxl qxl qxl qxl qxl qxl qxl qxl qxl qxl qxl qxl qxl qxl qxl qxl qxl qxl qxl qxl qxl qxl qxl qxl qxl qxl qxl qxl	hxp hxp hxp hxp hxp hxp hxp hxp hxp hxp hxp hxp hxp hxp hxp hxp hxp hxp hxp hxp hxp hxp hxp hxp hxp hxp hxp hxp

Typography

10/12	10/13
fmj fmj fmj fmj fmj fmj fmj fmj	hng hng hng hng hng hng hng
fmj fmj fmj fmj fmj fmj fmj fmj	hng hng hng hng hng hng hng
fmj fmj fmj fmj fmj fmj fmj fmj	hng hng hng hng hng hng hng
fmj fmj fmj fmj fmj fmj fmj fmj	hng hng hng hng hng hng hng

Line Length

Prior to the invention of printing, scribes laboriously copied manuscripts by hand. Because paper was very expensive, they paid special attention to filling each line with as many words as possible. All of their lines were carefully written to be of consistent length. Early printers imitated this style, and the practice of justifying lines remains a strong tradition today.

How long a line should be depends upon the typeface being used, the point size, and the leading. All of these factors influence how easy the type is to read—the readability. Beatrice Warde, the typographer, has estimated that the ideal line length is ten to twelve English words. Each word is considered to be five letters followed by a space, making the ideal line length between 50 to 60 characters, regardless of point size.

Physical Elements of Type Design

Type can be found almost everywhere we look: on store windows, and in buses, on candy wrappers and frozen foods, on billboards and tax forms, on money and even on aspirin. The proper use of type begins with some attention to the smallest parts of letters, and some special terms used by typographers.

The arm of a character is a horizontal projection or short upward sloping stroke:

A bar is an enclosed horizontal stroke:

The stem is the main part of the letter:

A cross stroke is that part of the letter which cuts across the stem:

t f

The tail is a downward projection:

K Q R

The apex is the uppermost point or where the stems come together.

A W

The vertex is the lowermost point where the stems join:

V

The ear is the projection found on certain lower case "g's:"

g

And, finally, the spur is the finishing stroke on certain upper case "G's:"

G

There are literally thousands of different type designs, and typographers speak of the unique characteristics of these typefaces using such words as "stem," "arm," "tail," etc.

The collection of all of the letters of the alphabet (A,B,C,a,b,c...), marks of punctuation (.,;:?!"...), marks of reference (°,†,‡,§...), commercial and monetary signs (%, #, $,...), mathematical signs (÷,=,+, × ...), and special characters (®, ©, • ...) comprise the font. Fonts vary in size from the basic alphabet, to well over one hundred characters. A complete font is shown.

Typography

uppercase or CAPITAL	ABCDEFGHIJKLMNOPQRSTUVWXYZ
lower case	abcdefghijklmnopqrstuvwxyz
SMALL CAPITALS	ABCDEFGHIJKLMNOPQRSTUVWXYZ
F LIGATURES	ff fi fl ffi ffl
FIGURES	1234567890
FRACTIONS	⅓ ⅓ ½ ¾ ¼
POINTS, OR THE MARKS OF PUNCTUATION	,."!;:-!)([]&?
MARKS OF REFERENCE	¶ § † ‡
COMMERCIAL AND MONETARY SIGNS	$ # %
SUPERIOR FIGURES	A^{1234567890}
SPECIAL CHARACTERS (sorts — not a normal part of the font)	© ® •
mathematical signs	÷ = + × /

Single Face Variations

When setting type, it is common practice to deal with different elements of a page layout in different ways. Headlines or other composition which separates text should be set so that they stand out. Words in text which are to be emphasized also require special attention. It is possible to meet these needs by using variations of a single type design.

Understanding Phototypesetting

Routine typesetting involves the use of capital and lower case letters. Two obvious variations are all capital composition and all lower case composition.

ALL CAPITAL COMPOSITION HIDES THE SHAPE OF INDIVIDUAL LETTERS

all lower case letters are much easier to read

Traditionally, printers have used the italic and boldface forms for emphasis. It is standard practice with phototypesetting fonts to purchase either the italic or the boldface to complement the main face.

Italic catches a reader's eye.

Boldface should be used only for emphasis.

A less common single-face variation is the use of small caps. Small caps, as the name implies, are capital letters which have a lower cap line than the normal capital letters.

SMALL CAPITALS ARE LESS COMMONLY USED.

Type size is probably the most common method of varying the appearance of a typeface. Phototypesetting systems differ in their range of available point sizes; but they can, in general, set sizes as small as 5 points and as large as 72.

The larger the point size the more attention it gets. The relative size is equal to the relative importance of the com-

Typeface Geometry

Typographic characters are composed to form straight lines of type. Each letter in a line rests on an imaginary base line.

The upper line below which the main part of all lower case letters are located is called the mean line.

The distance between the base line and the mean line is called the "x" height, because it is the height of the lower case x. Typefaces with large x heights are usually easier to read.

Lower case letters which descend or dip below the base line (g,j,p,q,y) are called descenders. The lowermost point of a descender is the descender line.

Lower case letters which ascend or project upward (b,d,f,h,k,l,t) are called ascenders. The uppermost point of an ascender is the ascender or cap line.

Typesetting systems which provide for mixing two or more type sizes in a single line are either base or center aligning. Base aligning systems have all sizes sitting on the base line. Center aligning systems have all sizes centered between the base line and ascender line of the largest type size.

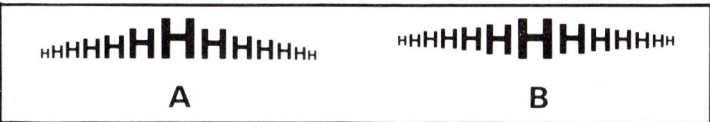

Figure 7. A base-aligning character system shown in A, a center-aligning system in B.

Type Classification

Printers have devised many methods of classifying typefaces. Only the basic categories will be covered here.

A typeface either has or does not have serifs. Serifs are ending strokes on the arms, stems, and tails of some typeface designs. If a typeface has serifs it is termed a roman typeface. A typeface design without (sans) serifs is termed a sans serif.

Typefaces which slant forward are called italic.

Italic

However, any typeface which stands upright in comparison to an italic is called a roman. This is somewhat confusing since both roman and sans serif typefaces have italic forms.

The earliest typefaces, those from the Gutenberg workshop, were copies of the letterforms found in handwritten manuscripts. As a group, they are called *Blackletter*, a version of which is referred to as *Old English*. These letters appear heavy, ornate, and have angular serifs.

𝔅𝔩𝔞𝔠𝔨𝔩𝔢𝔱𝔱𝔢𝔯

Printing from movable type spread from Germany south to Italy, and there the classical letterforms of Humanist manuscripts became the models for the *roman* typefaces. The earliest roman forms were called "old style."

Roman

The roman forms underwent many changes during the interim period from approximately 1470 to 1775. In that year Giambattista Bodoni introduced a type design of mechanical structure, with heavy stems and light serifs. It is classified as a *modern* typeface.

Modern

About the turn of the nineteenth century, a new commercial interest in type design began. One result of that attention was a group of type designs called *square serifs*.

Square Serif

Typography

In 1816, William Caslon IV designed a typeface with no serifs. This was itself an innovation of major proportions. This was the first *sans serif* typeface, the first of many, and the beginning of a major classification.

Sans Serif

Typefaces imitating handwriting were first used in the sixteenth century. They appear to be drawn with pen and ink and are classified as *scripts* and *cursives*. The letters of a script typeface are joined; the letters of a cursive typeface are not.

Script

Typefaces which do not fit any of the previous classifications may be grouped in a category called *decorative* or *display*.

Decorative

The Parts of a Page

The area which most type is destined to occupy is the *page*. A few of the more common elements of page make-up follow:

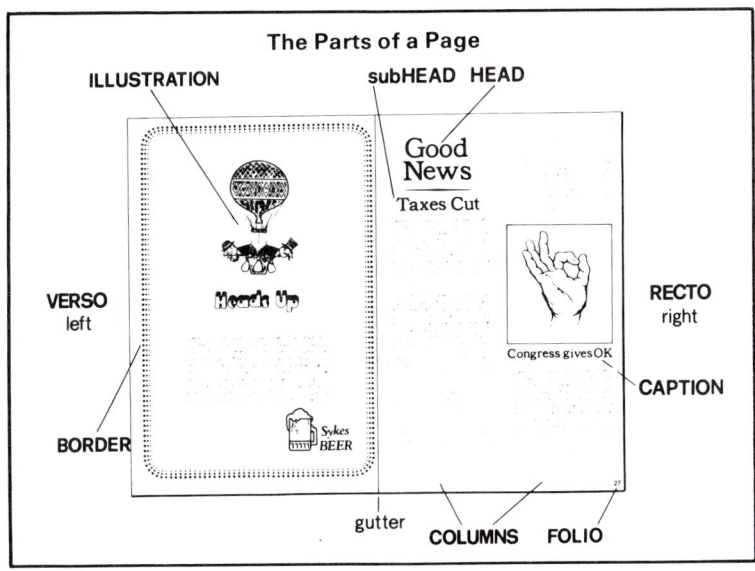

Illustration - a picture or diagram used to clarify the message presented in the text.

Border - either a simple or fancy design used to frame a page for decoration, or to set apart blocks of typematter.

Gutter - blank space between pages or between columns of type.

Head (Headline) - the display line at the "head" or beginning of an ad, chapter, page, or book.

Subhead (sub-headline) - a subordinate headline carrying information of secondary importance.

Caption - lines of text positioned by or under a picture or illustration which explain or describe it.

Columns - the lengthwise arrangement of lines of type.

Folio - a page number.

Verso - the left-hand side of a two-page spread. Verso pages are always even-numbered.

Recto - the right-hand side of a two-page spread. Recto pages are always odd-numbered.

Legibility and Readability

A type designer is responsible for making his type design legible; that is, drawing each character so that it clearly depicts the letterform which it is meant to represent. The printer's use of the typeface determines its readability; how easy it is to read on the printed page. Here are a few guidelines for making type easier to read:

Do

Use approximately 20% of the type size for leading.
Use a minimum of wordspacing.
Use a 10 or 12 point typeface for text matter.
Select a typeface to suit the intended use.
Break words according to pronunciation.
Use *italic* and **boldface** for emphasis.

Do Not

Use ornate typefaces for text.
Use a too long or too short line measure.
Use all capital composition in text.
Use all capital composition for any blackletter or script type.
Use excessive letter or word spacing.
Use condensed or expanded typefaces for reading matter.

2 photolettering machines

Summary

The *photolettering machine* is a variety of phototypesetter used to set display sizes of type. Some of these machines are termed *blind* because they do not allow for the examination of type as it is being set. Other machines are called *visual* due to the fact that the operator can see each letter as it is being composed.

Photolettering machines are unique in many of the styles of composition that they are capable of setting. Such special effects as *bouncing, staggering, curving, screening,* and *shadowing* are all possible using one or more photolettering devices.

The method used to expose a negative film font to light sensitive material may be by either *contacting* the two, or by *projecting* the character image (font) through a lens and onto the photographic paper or film. When the letter is contacted it remains at the size appearing on the font itself (100%), whereas projected images can be enlarged and reduced.

Keyboard machines which let the operator key-in the copy on a typewriter-like device, are the fastest photolettering machines, yet do not have the versatility for setting special typographic effects.

Other cold-type methods of setting display type include a pantographic-like device using pen and ink (Varigraph), the manual assembly of laterally reversed, white-on-black letters for photographing on a darkroom camera (Kameratype), and the transferring of specially printed letters from plastic carrier sheets onto paper (transfer type).

Trade Terms

backslant - letters which lean to the left, just as italic letters lean to the right.

blind machine - a photolettering device which does not permit the operator to view the composition until after it has been processed.

bounce - a form of letter arrangement wherein the characters are set in an alternating up-down-up style.

cassette - a container for holding exposed photographic material.

condensed - a typeface which is narrower than the normal.

contact - a method of photographic exposure whereby the film negative and the light-sensitive material touch.

curve - type set along the arc of a circle giving a round, semi-circular effect.

daylight operating - referring to a photolettering machine which does not require a darkroom, or safelight conditions.

display - referring to point sizes larger than 14 points.

expanded - a typeface which is wider than normal in comparison with its height.

italic - a type form which slopes forward and to the right, approximately 15 degrees or more from the perpendicular.

keyboard machine - a photolettering machine which uses a typewriter-like device to key-in the characters to be set.

laterally reversed - a mirror image.

mix - the use of more than one typeface or size within a single word or line.

overlap - letters which are partially set over one another.

photolettering - the setting of display size type, in any of its various forms, by photographic means.

pi font - a collection of special characters, symbols, and ornaments, not appearing in the standard font.

projection - a method of photographic exposure whereby a lens is placed between the film negative (font) and the photographic material. Adjustment of the distance between the font and the lens, and the light-sensitive material and the lens results in changes in the size of the projected image (image size—enlargement or reduction).

right reading - composition appearing in proper reading form, i.e. reading from left to right.

screen - a patterned sheet or strip of film which is exposed in contact with a font to produce letters with a textured, shaded, or decorated appearance.

shadow - a typeface variation used to achieve a three-dimensional effect by appearing as a cast shadow.

stack - single letters, or lines of type, set one upon the other.

stagger - letters set at alternating forward and backward slants.

step and repeat - a single character or design which is repeatedly set at equidistant steps to produce a border or a piece of decorative typography.

step up - step down - letters of a word or words increasing (step up) or decreasing (step down) at fixed percentages to produce a three dimensional effect.

text - referring to type sizes smaller than 14 points, i.e. those sizes used for reading matter.

visual machine - a photolettering machine which permits the operator to view either the actual type he is composing, or a reasonable facsimile thereof.

Introduction

Type sizes larger than 14 points are usually classified as display, while smaller sizes used for reading matter are called text. Traditionally, typesetting machines have been designed to set one or the other: text or display. In hot metal typesetting, for example, a Linotype machine might be used to set text and a Ludlow machine would be used to set display.

While most phototypesetting systems can set a complete range of type sizes, a distinct category of phototypesetting is the photolettering machine. It is usually manually operated rather than tape-driven, and produces a continuous strip of 35mm. or 2-inch paper or film, rather than justified lines of text. Machines of this type may be of the contact variety—one type font for each size, or the projection variety, where each font may be enlarged or reduced to produce a range of sizes. Furthermore, the machine may require a darkroom for exposure and processing or may be operated in roomlight conditions.

Selection of a photolettering machine is usually based upon a choice between speed of production and flexibility of output. Speed is related to the ease by which letters can be located, positioned, exposed, and processed; and flexibility refers to the range of sizes and special effects which can be produced.

History

One of the first references to a photolettering machine appears in an 1856 British patent. Some accounts, however, credit the first machine to Eugen Prozsolt of Budapest. In 1894, he introduced a typewriter-like keyboard which, when struck, elevated a letter into photographing position. Shortly

Figure 1. The A.E. Bawtree photographic type-composing machine.

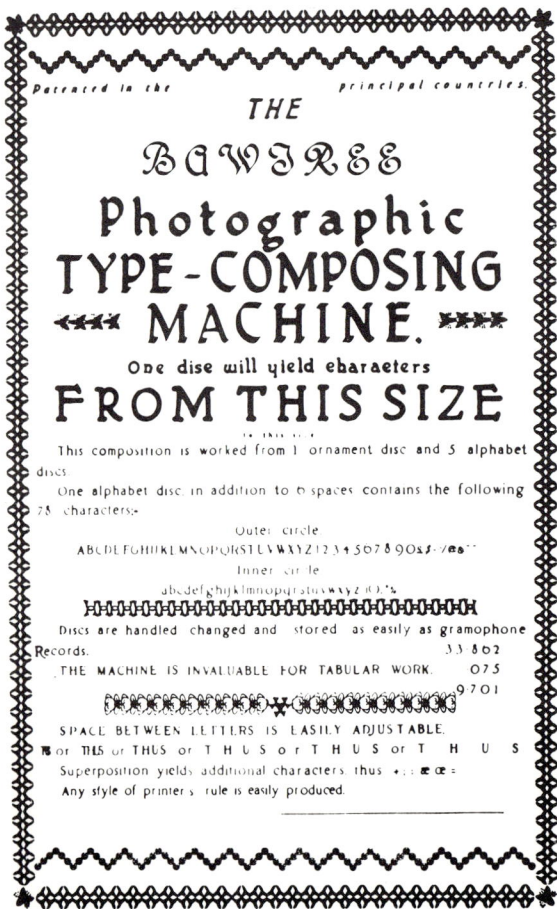
Figure 2. An advertisement for, and by, the Bawtree photographic type-composing machine.

thereafter, in 1898, W. Friese-Greene of London, developed a machine using strips of letters, arranged in order of width. As keys were touched, letters were assembled and presented before a camera for photographing.

In 1915, A.E. Bawtree, introduced his "photographic type-composing machine," as shown in Figure 1. It was based on the original 1856 British patent, with characters arranged in circular fashion on a negative disc. An example of its versatility is shown in Figure 2. According to Bawtree, "it is not suggested that the machine will supersede such inventions as the Monotype or Linotype. It is not intended nor is it suitable for masses of cheap type work, such as newspapers and ordinary books. For all display work, for books which are to be printed in special type and for titles and descriptive matter, the method here set forth is very advantageous..."

In the years which followed, there were many innovations in photolettering or display phototypesetting. This interest was due in great part to the growth of the lithographic printing process, which uses photomechanical methods to produce printing surfaces. Type set photographically was, and still is, a compatible and important part of the lithographic production cycle.

Photolettering Techniques

There are two basic forms which composition from a photolettering machine may take. First is the straight line of proportionally spaced characters as shown.

Cigarettes can take your breath away.

This form of composition, regardless of the machine used to set it, is usually the fastest, limited only by the time it takes to locate and expose each character. In most cases, the machine operator uses reference marks on a font film strip or disc, or some calibrated machine setting.

The second form of composition involves any one or more of several typographic techniques. These are the special effects which are almost completely unique to photolettering machines. These effects are usually more time consuming since they may involve multiple exposures, repositioning of lenses or photographic materials, changing fonts, inserting screen patterns, or otherwise modifying a machine. Some of the more common lettering variations follow.

Letters set in an up-down-up style, similar to the movement of a rubber ball dropped on a pavement, are said to *bounce*. Bouncing letters give the appearance of movement and activity.

Understanding Phototypesetting

Letters which lean to the right at a slight degree and sit on a common baseline are called *italic*. By using distortion lenses some photolettering machines can convert an upright (roman) letter font to a representation of an italic form.

upright *italic*

The opposite of an italic is a *backslant*. In this case the letters slant backward at a slight degree while also sitting on a common baseline.

backslant

A variation of both the italic and the backslant is the *stagger*. Letters are set at alternating forward and backward angles off the baseline.

STAGGER

Letters can also be optically modified through the use of distortion lenses. In this way a single font can take on many variations from *condensed* to *expanded*. The example below shows the effects possible with two Phototypositor distortion lenses. Remember that all of these variations are from a single type font.

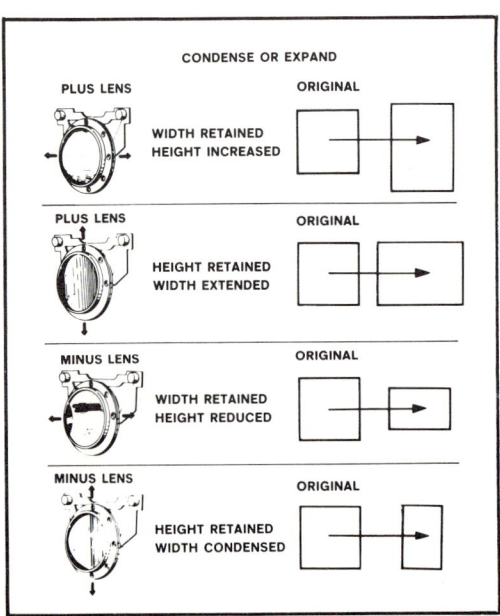

Most photolettering machines allow for the changing of fonts at any point during composition. In this way it is possible to mix two or more type fonts in a single word or line.

Q‍uiet!

The closer than normal spacing of letters to achieve a more pleasing appearance is called kerning. Taken to an extreme, kerning becomes overlapping, where one letter enters the space of a neighboring letter.

Kerning Overlapping

Letters which sit on the arc of a circle are said to curve. Some photolettering machines are capable of setting 360-degree circles.

Lettergraphics International Inc.

Many different screen patterns can be exposed in contact with a type font to produce a variety of shadings, textures and designs.

Shhhhhhh!

A font may also be repeatedly exposed—with a screen and non-screen exposure to produce a shadow effect.

SHADOW

Machines which use the projection principle are capable of changing type size. These machines can set step up-step down composition.

If a machine is capable of setting multiple lines, that is, more than one line along the vertical dimension of the photographic material, then it is also probably capable of stacking. Stacking is the closer than normal spacing of lines (or parts of lines) of type.

DON'T BLOW YOUR STACK

Single characters of a font, or special designs made in the format (strip, disc, slide) of the machine, may be exposed at evenly spaced intervals to make a border. The process of exposing the same image over and over is called step and repeat.

⨀⨀⨀⨀⨀⨀⨀⨀⨀

✸✸✸✸✸✸✸✸✸

Finally, any number of different methods can be used together to produce a piece of custom typography.

The Blind Machines

Photolettering machines which do not allow for the visual examination of characters as they are being set are called blind machines. Machines of this kind usually rely on control settings or font reference points rather than the typographic skill of the operator. One of the first commercially successful photolettering machines in this category was the *Filmotype*° machine.

The Filmotype machine uses 2-inch wide negative film fonts wound on reels and mounted under one of two handles, as shown in Figure 3. As the handles are turned the required characters are positioned, and one-by-one exposed in contact to photographic paper or film. The exposed material is then fed into a light-tight cassette. When the necessary composition is complete, the cassette is removed from the machine and its contents are processed in a table-top processor, also made by Filmotype. All operations are in daylight.

°*Alphatype Corp., 7500 McCormick Blvd., Skokie, IL 60076*

Photolettering Machines

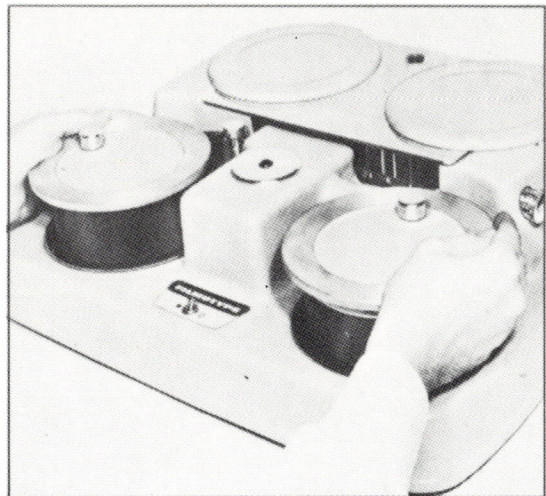

Figure 3. *The Filmotype photolettering machine uses the contact principle to compose characters from 2-inch film fonts.*

The Filmotype	
Category	blind
Model	———
Approx. cost	$800°
Font cost	$18
Method of exposure	contact
Point size availability	6 pt. - 96 pt.
Character positioning	reference marks
Processing	external, processor $225
Special effects	intermixing, letterspacing, reverses, borders, screen patterns, shadow effects.

°*Prices are shown to give the reader a base of comparison. The author accepts no responsibility for price changes.*

Understanding Phototypesetting

The *StripPrinter*° (Figure 4) is one of the lowest-cost photolettering machines in use today. Each 35mm. mylar film font has two reference marks for each character, a beginning and ending line indicating the width of the character. The character to be exposed is positioned in reference to a stationary scale on the machine's working surface, beneath which is 35mm. photographic paper or film. The character's beginning reference mark is aligned with the zero reading on the scale. The locking lever is pulled forward securing the font and the paper together. The lever is then pushed to the left until the character's ending reference mark is aligned with the zero. The movement of the lever reveals a width of paper equal to the width of the character. The exposure button is depressed and a preset amount of timed light exposes the paper. The locking lever is then released and returned to the right. This procedure is repeated for each character to be set.

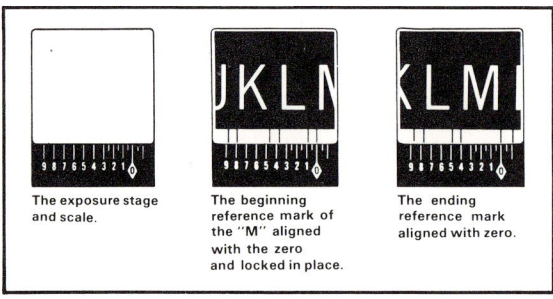

The exposure stage and scale.

The beginning reference mark of the "M" aligned with the zero and locked in place.

The ending reference mark aligned with zero.

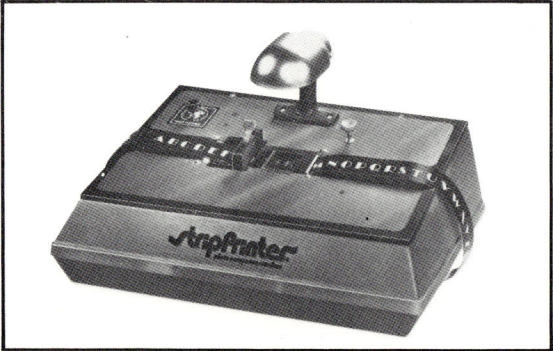

Figure 4. The low-cost StripPrinter is a blind contact photolettering machine.

°*StripPrinter Inc., P.O. Box 18895, Oklahoma City, OK 73118*

Photolettering Machines

The StripPrinter	
Category	Blind
Model	300
Approx. cost	$350
Font cost	$6
Font size	35mm.
Method of exposure	contact
Point size availability	6 pt. - 96 pt.
Character positioning	reference marks
Processing	external manual
Special effects	intermixing, kerning reverses, screen patterns, scripts.

    The VariTyper division of the Addressograph-Multigraph Corporation markets the *Headliner°*, available in two models. Each machine uses the round plexiglas Headliner typemaster fonts with characters arranged in circular fashion. Grooves cut along the circumference correspond to character width; the wider the character, the deeper the groove. Figure 5 shows a typemaster being positioned on the model 860. The typemaster also has an inner circle of reference characters, each positioned diametrically opposite its its

°*Addressograph-Multigraph Corporation, 11 Mt. Pleasant Ave., East Hanover, NJ 07936*

negative counterpart. When the reference character appears between two register marks on the face of the machine, the negative image is positioned under a light-tight hood and over a strip of 35mm. film or paper. When the print switch is pushed a lever senses the depth of the character's groove, and moves the photographic material the appropriate distance. The material is then exposed to a variable intensity light.

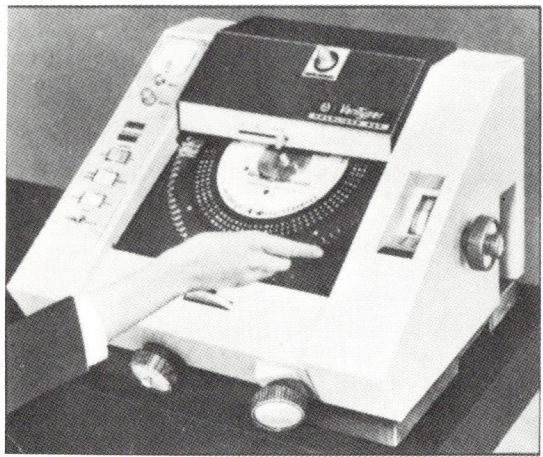

Figure 5. A typemaster being placed on a Headline 860 photolettering machine.

The Headliner

Category	blind
Model	820
Approx. cost	$2025
Font cost	$55
Font size	13½" disc
Method of exposure	contact
Point size availability	10 pt-84 pt
Character positioning	reference characters
Processing	internal
Special effects	reverses, screens, kerning

Photolettering Machines

Model	860
Approx. cost	$2350
Font cost	$65
Font size	13½" disc
Method of exposure	contact
point size availability	NA
Character positioning	reference characters
Processing	internal
Special effects	setting multiple lines (up to 5) 35 mm. strip

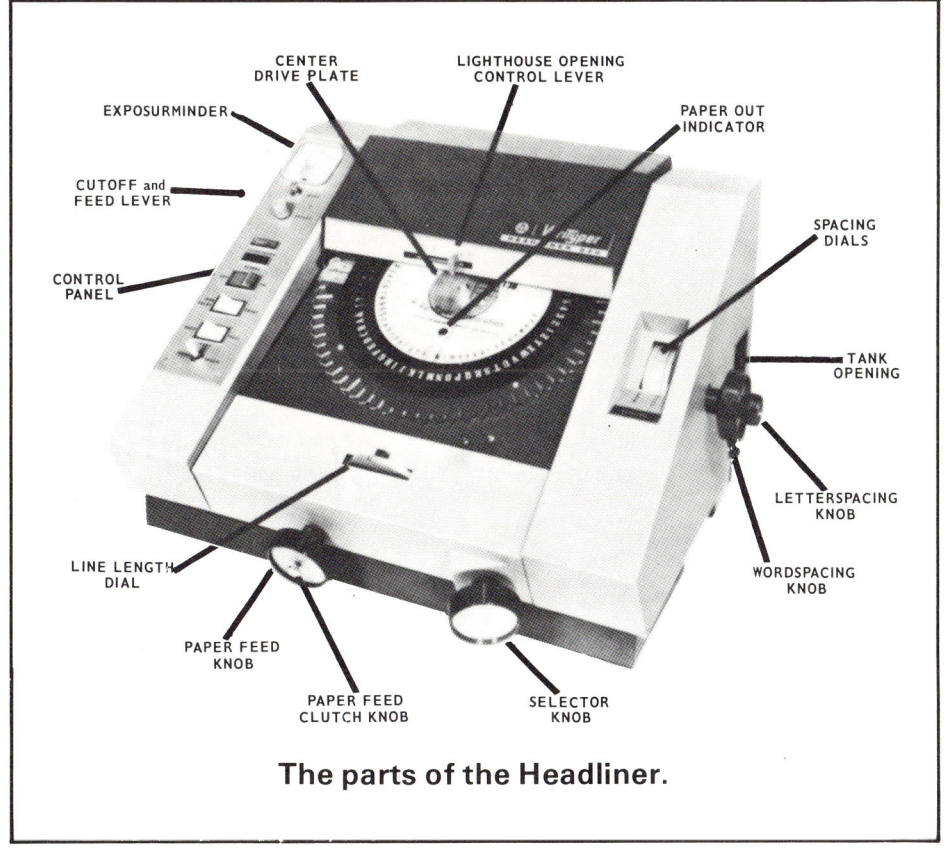

The parts of the Headliner.

The Visual Machines

Photolettering machines which either let the operator see exactly what he is composing, or else give some representation of what he has set are called visual machines. One of the first, and certainly among the most popular, is Visual Graphic Corporation's *Phototypositor*.° Originally designed to use the 2-inch Filmotype film fonts, the Phototypositor now boasts one of the largest font libraries of any photolettering machine manufacturer.

The Phototypositor uses the projection principle, rather than contacting the font directly to the paper. It is similar in some ways to a darkroom enlarger, in that one filmstrip, like one photo negative, can be enlarged or reduced to a variety of sizes—in this case from a reduction of 25% to an enlargement of 200%. This means that a font which measures 72 points at 100% can not only be reduced to 18 points and enlarged to 144 points, but can be set to any size in between.

The operating theory of the Phototypositor is quite simple. A small rectangular piece of clear plexiglas is located over a portion of 2-inch wide photographic material (paper or film). Between the plexiglas (developer cell) and the photographic material, there is a layer of developer. To the left of this there are two other cells with layers of a two-stage stop bath. This is all enclosed in a light-tight frame with a viewing hood. A yellow light behind the font projects a character through a lens and onto the developer-laden paper. The paper is not sensitive to yellow light. The operator has complete visual control over the positioning of the character. Once satisfactorily positioned, the exposure lever is depressed. A mirror which had reflected the yellow light, then swings out of the way so that a high intensity white light can expose the sensitive paper. At the same time more developer and stop bath are automatically fed into the cells. Rubber coated gripper fingers are used to grab the paper and push it out of the machine where it is fixed.

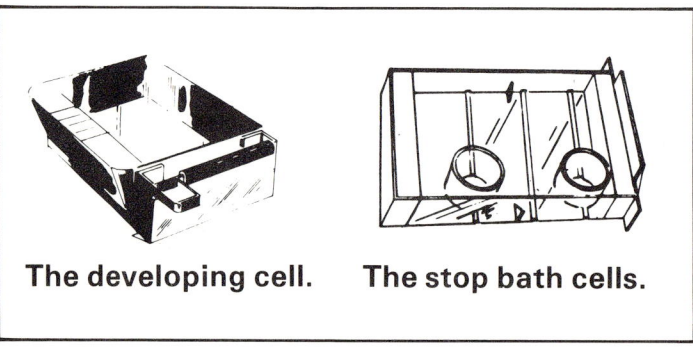

The developing cell.   **The stop bath cells.**

°*Visual Graphic Corporation, 1400 N.E. 125 St., N. Miami, FL 33161*

Photolettering Machines

Figure 6. The Phototypositor is a visual projection photolettering machine.

The Phototypositor

Category	visual
Model	3000
Approx. cost	$3300
Font cost	generally under $45
Font size	2"
Method of exposure	projection
Point size availability	18 pt-144 pt. inclusive
Character positioning	manual, visual
Processing	internal development and stop bath, external fixing
Special effects	curves, stagger, bounce, screen, step down - step up, mixing, multiple lines, scripts, step and repeat, condense, expand, circular setting (opt)

The *Copytype*° is a West German machine made by Dr. Boger Photosatz. It uses a double lens system, projecting an image on both the photographic material and on a fluorescent foil composition board. The image on the composing foil glows, showing the operator his exact position in relation to the photographic material. As the type is set, the photographic material is fed into a light-tight cassette. When the composition is complete, the cassette is removed and its contents are processed.

The Copytype	
Category	visual
Model	250
Approx. cost	$2000, daylight adapter $500 2" font adapter $500
Font cost	$60
Font size	2" film or rigid plastic
Method of exposure	projection
Point size availability	reductions of 50% up to enlargements of 1500%
Character positioning	manual and visual
Processing	external processors $300-$450
Special effects	multiple lines, mixing, screens, optional optical modifier

Model	500
Approx. cost	$3000
Font cost	$60/strip
Font size	2" film or rigid plastic
Method of exposure	projection
Point size availability	up to 144 pts inclusive
Character positioning	manual and visual
Processing	external processors $300-$450
Special effects	multiple lines, mixing, screens, optional optical modifier

°*Dr. Bögen Photosatz OMBH, 2 Wedel In Holstein, Rissemer Strasse 94, Germany*

Photolettering Machines

Figure 7. The Copytype (formerly Visutek) displays characters on a glowing foil composition board.

Like the Filmotype and the Phototypositor, the Copytype uses 2-inch film fonts and is daylight operating. However, it does boast a wider range of typefaces and sizes since it also accepts European plastic film strip fonts and has a projection system capable of sizes as small as 50% reductions and as large as 1500% enlargements.

The *Staromat Display Typesetter*° is a German machine manufactured by Berthold Fototype Company. Unlike any of the previously mentioned machines, the Staromat requires a darkroom. This is due to the fact that the photographic paper or film must be pre-activated by a 30 second bath in a tray of developer. The photographic material is then placed on a setting table similar to a photographic enlarging easel. This table is positioned beneath the Staromat projection head, which resembles a photographic enlarger. The setting table permits precision movement of the photographic material, left or right, up or down, or at any angle.

The Staromat accommodates either a rigid plastic film font, or with a special adapter, 2-inch fonts, as used on the Filmotype and Phototypositor. The font is placed in the projection head, and the selected character is projected through a red filter onto the setting table. Since the pre-activated paper is not sensitive to red light, the character can be safely and visibly maneuvered until in the proper position. Once positioned, a push button or foot switch is

°*Berthold Fototype Company, P.O. Box 430, 59 Willet St., Bloomfield, NJ 07003*

activated, the red filter is automatically swung aside, and white light exposes the photographic material. The image develops instantly, and the red filter is automatically brought back into position for locating the next character. When setting is complete the material is re-activated, fixed, and washed.

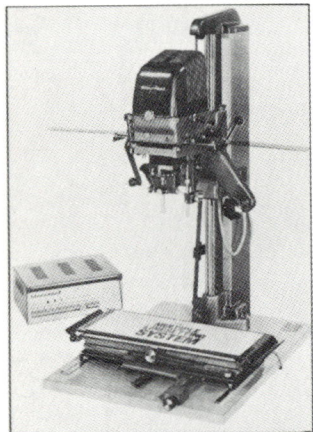

Figure 8. The Staromat Display Typesetter is a modified darkroom enlarger.

The Staromat	
Category	visual
Model	————
Approx. cost	$3600
Font cost	rigid plastic fonts $70 2" film strips $20
Font size	2" film strip or rigid plastic
Method of exposure	projection
Point size availability	24 pts to 5-½ with attachments 6 pt-6 feet
Character positioning	manual and visual
Processing	external with trays
Special effects	multiple lines mixing, screens, circular, distortions, 12 fixed modification forms, use as an enlarger

Photolettering Machines

The Keyboard Machines

Machines which use a typewriter-like device for locating characters of display type are classified as keyboard machines. These machines are among the fastest for the production of continuous strips of display type. Like the manual machines, there are both visual and blind models, yet unlike the manual machines there are few special effects obtainable.

One popular photolettering keyboard machine is the *Compugraphic CG 7200°*. It features keyboard control of character selection, and automatic locating and exposing of each character to 35mm. photographic material. An electronic visual display unit is available as an option. Flexibility of output is limited to four typefaces and eight type sizes, as well as controlled letter and word spacing.

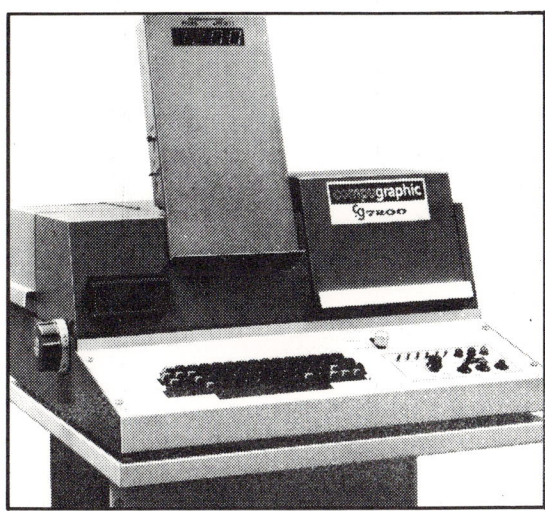

The CG 7200

The ExecuWriter Display

°*Compugraphic Corp., 80 Industrial Way, Wilmington, MA 01887*

Understanding Phototypesetting

The *ExecuWriter Display* by Compugraphic is the lowest cost keyboarding-activated display typesetter made today. One fixed size, low cost duplexed film strip is available within the machine providing two typefaces, either accessible at the flip of a switch. The machine provides for letter and word spacing and with special fonts is capable of producing scripts, outlines, italics, and reverses. The output is 16mm, photographic paper or film which is processed external to the machine.

	The CG 7200
Category	keyboard
Model	7200L
Approx. cost	$3650, visual character display. + $1800
Font cost	$60
Method of exposure	projection
Point size availability	14,18,24,30,36,48,60,72
Character positioning	keyboard
Processing	external
Special effects for both	mixing, kerning, variable letterspacing, wordspacing, overlapping

Model	7200H
Approx. cost	$4450
Font cost	$60
Method of exposure	projection
Point size availability	30,36,48,60,72,84,96,120
Character positioning	keyboard
Processing	external

The *Singer Photo Display 70*° is a blind keyboard machine. Unlike the CG 7200, which has a one line buffer, or storage, the Photo Display 70 locates and exposes each character as it is keyed. This limits the speed of operation,

°*The Singer Co., 151 Callan Ave., San Leandro, CA 94577*

Photolettering Machines

especially for larger sizes which require slower machine rhythm. The machine features a 56 character pi font in addition to four 92 character type fonts. A pi font is a collection of special characters not usually found in even a complete font. This machine like the CG 7200 can be operated by anyone with only minutes of instruction.

The Singer Photo Display 70

Category	keyboard
Model	70
	70T copy can be shortened or lengthened to fill a measure
Approx. cost	$4550
	$6400
Font cost	$100
Method of exposure	projection
Point size availability	12,18,24,30,36,48,60,72,96
Character positioning	keyboard
Processing	external
Special effects	mixing, kerning, variable letterspacing and wordspacing, overlapping

Other Cold Type Methods

The Varigraph. The Varigraph is a mechanical typesetting instrument, based on the pantograph principle. The tracing point is guided through the appropriate engraving on a type matrix. The tracing point is linked to a pen with a

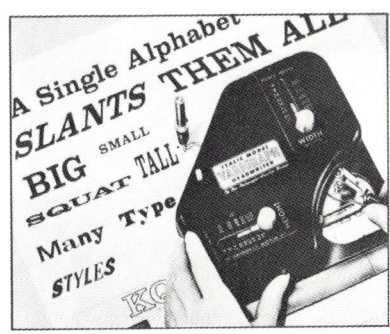

The Varigraph

reservoir of india ink. As the tracing point follows the outline of each letter, the pen draws the letter on paper. By altering the linkage between the tracing point and the pen, hundreds of variations of size and shape can be achieved.

The Varigraph

Category	mechanical
Model	office model
	italic model
Approx. cost	$160
	$190
Font cost	$16-29
Method of exposure	non-photographic
Point size availability	14 pt-72 pt
Character positioning	manual
Processing	non-photographic
Special effects	outlines, reverses, expand, condense, step, shadow, curve, borders

Kameratype. Kameratype uses the principle of hand composition to set type with the use of a darkroom camera. Each character is formed in white on a precision-cut rectangle of 1/16" thick black plastic. The characters measure 96 points and are laterally reversed (mirror images). After they are set from right to left in a special composing stick (channel guide), they are placed on the copy board of a darkroom camera and photographed onto paper or film. The result is right-reading phototypesetting. The size range is limited only by the capabilities of the camera being used.

The Kameratype

Photolettering Machines

The Kameratype

Category	manual
Model	———
Approx. cost	24" composing stick $3 30" composing stick $3.50
Font cost	single font (340 char.) $58.50 double font (680 char.) $98.50
Method of exposure	process camera
Point size availability	dependent upon camera
Character positioning	manual
Processing	stabilization or conventional
Special effects	mixing

Transfer Type. Transfer type is the name given to any form of pressure-sensitive material carrying typographic characters. This includes methods where the character is directly burnished onto paper, or first cut out of a carrier sheet and then burnished onto paper or board. Such products include Formatt, C-Thru Lettering, Chartpak, Instantype, Letraset, ATF Spectype, Prestype, and others.

Distortion Optics. Type set by *any* method can be converted by special optical systems into special effect typography with the use of a darkroom camera. Graphic Developments Incorporated of Chicago markets a number of lenses which can distort straight line typography into pop art, expanded or condensed, concave or convex, spheroid, angled, wavy, or completely circular form.

Graphic Developments

Category	distortion optics
Model	9020
Approx. cost	$500
Special effects	completely circular composition
Model	9030
Approx. cost	$350
Special effects	carnival mirror effects
Model	9040
Approx. cost	$140
Special effects	concave/convex
Model	9060
Approx cost	$400
Special effects	condense/expand

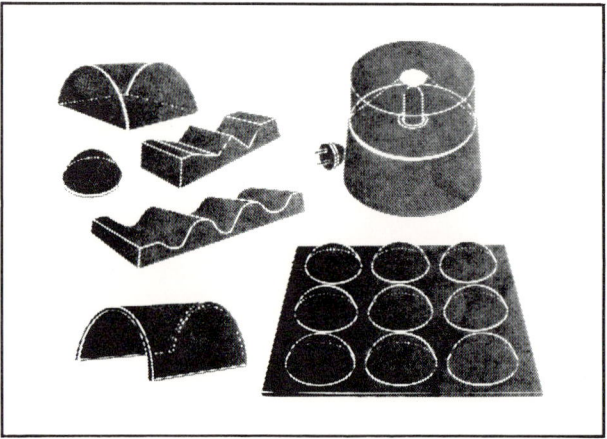

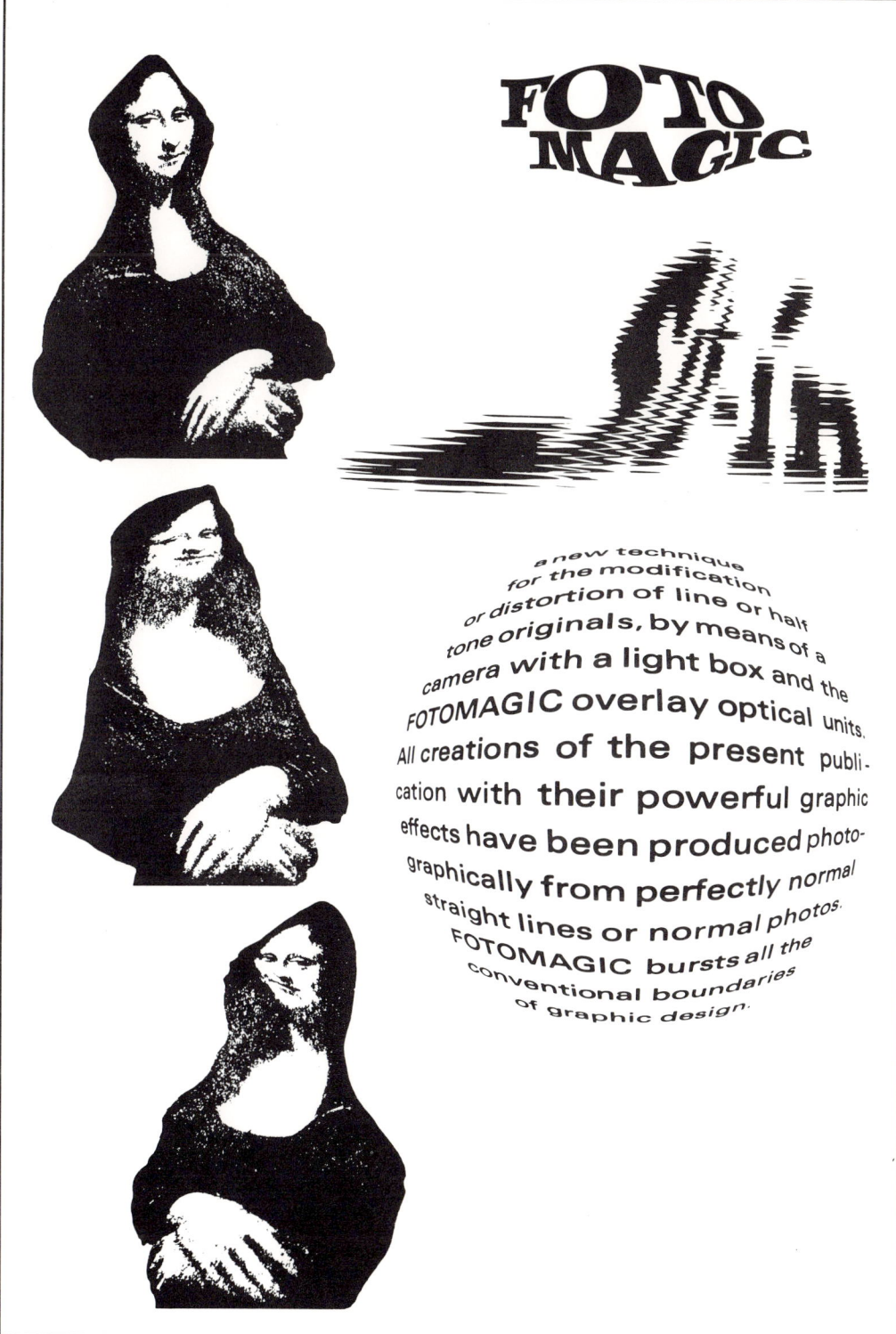

3 direct impression typesetting

Summary

Direct impression typesetting is a method of composing, reproduction quality type from a device resembling a typewriter. Two machines account for most of the direct impression typesetting produced today: the VariTyper, made by the Addressograph-Multigraph Corporation, and the Selectric Composer, made by the International Business Machines Corporation.

    To achieve a typeset rather than typewritten appearance of its output, the direct impression machine has specific methods and devices for changing typeface, type size, and leading, altering letterspacing, and performing quadding and justification. Unlike standard office typewriters, which are built with uniform character spacing (pica or elite), direct impression machines have *proportional spacing*, producing properly (at at least better) letterspaced characters.

    Justification requires two typings: the first to measure how short the line is from the end of the measure, and the second to distribute that excess between words to *space out* the line.

    Direct impression typesetting is a development of the use of a standard typewriter to produce type for mimeographing. As office and small shop methods of graphic reproduction improved, a better quality image was needed. Refinements in the typewriter resulted in the direct impression machine, and it became the logical low-cost alternative to the Linotype, Monotype, and expensive phototypesetting.

Trade Terms

cold-type composition - generally referring to type which is set by other than hot metal methods, but specifically relating to type set on a direct impression device.

direct image typesetting - see direct impression typesetting.

direct impression typesetting - typographic composition produced by a special purpose typewriter.

direct entry phototypesetting - operation of a phototypesetting photo unit by activation of an on-line keyboard.

elite - a fixed typewriter spacing system with 12 characters to the inch.

escapement - that part of a typewriter or direct impression machine which controls the letterspacing of characters, also the actual letterspacing of characters themselves.

fixed spacing - uniform letterspacing of all characters regardless of width.

horizontal spacing - fixed or variable letterspacing of characters. Also called escapement.

impact typesetting - see direct impression typesetting.

parallel justification - a method of double-typing-justification wherein the rough and justified lines are side-by-side (parallel).

pica - a fixed space typewriter system with 10 characters to the inch.

platen - the impression cylinder around which paper is held for typing.

proportional spacing - a typewriter spacing system wherein characters are letterspaced relative to their widths.

rule - a composed horizontal line, of various widths.

serial justification - a method of double-typing-justification wherein the rough lines are all typed first, then all of the justified lines are typed.

spacing out - a method of justification in which the space remaining at the end of a short line is equally distributed between words or characters in the line to expand it to fill the line measure.

strike-on typesetting - see direct impression typesetting.

type element - a piece of metal or plastic which carries a typeface on its surface. Direct impression machines allow for the quick change of elements to achieve different typeface size and styles.

typewriter - an office machine used to mechanically or electromechanically impress metal type characters on an inked ribbon to produce dark letters, in composed form, on paper.

vertical spacing - single, double, or half spacing on a typewriter, points of leading on a direct impression device.

Introduction

The idea for direct impression composition was first stated in 1714, by Mr. Henry Mill, an Englishman, who took out a patent for a machine which he described as "an artificial machine or method for impressing or transcribing of letters, singly or progressively, one after another as in writing, whereby all writings whatsoever may be engrossed in paper or parchment so neat and exact as not to be distinguished from print." Mill's machine failed however, but his idea obviously did not. In 1867, C. Latham Sholes and Samuel W. Soulé, printers in Milwaukee, and their associate, a Mister Carlos Glidden, continued development of what was to be known as the "type-writer." By 1873 they had completed a practical working machine which was manufactured, shortly thereafter, by E. Remington and Sons of Ilion, New York. The acceptance of the machine by business and industry stimulated other inventors to produce similar machines. Ironically, by 1884 the Central Type Foundry of Boston was producing a typeface called "Type-Writer," and the machine which had been invented to simulate printing, was now being simulated in print. It reportedly had a larger sale than any typeface ever before issued. According to one account, the design was suggested by a stationer from Huntingdon, Pennsylvania, Mr. J.C. Blair, who was reputedly a typographic expert. The typeface was sold with the intention that "circulars could be made to resemble genuine correspondence, and thus secure for them the attention which it was previously so hard to get." Today, most typesetting machines still offer a typeface which resembles typewritten characters. Figure 1 shows a typewriter font made by the Visual Graphics Corporation.

```
abcdeefghijklmnop
ABCDEFGHIJKLMNOP
1234567890 (&&.,:;!?"")
```

Figure 1. A modern typewriter font made by the Visual Graphics Corporation for the Phototypositor.

Direct impression, sometimes referred to as strike-on, direct image, or impact typesetting, uses a typewriter-like device for composing type characters directly onto paper. Unlike an ordinary office typewriter, it produces sharp, dense (black), proportionally spaced characters suitable for offset reproduction. There are only two major manufacturers of direct impression machines: Addressograph-Multigraph, makers of the VariTyper, and IBM, makers of the Selectric Composer.° All general statements concerning direct impression composition will relate to these two machines. (See Figure 2.)

°*The Composer is no longer made although reconditioned units are still sold.*

Direct Impression Typesetting

Figure 2. The AM VariTyper and the IBM Selectric Composer, the two representative direct impression typesetters.

Composition Components on Direct Impression Surfaces

Direct impression machines, like all typewriters, attempt to imitate hot metal typesetting. They do so by a number of sophisticated machine settings which control certain components of composition. Figure 3 shows a simple form which was produced on a direct impression machine. Some of the components of this and similar composition follow:

    A. *Typefaces.* The typefaces on direct impression machines are easily changed, although it is necessary that typing stop while a new type element is inserted into the machine. The VariTyper has a type library of over 1000 type

Understanding Phototypesetting

faces, with two type fonts located on each type plate. The IBM Composer has 130 fonts available, with one type design to each sphere-shaped element. (See Figure 4)

B. Type size. For each change of type size, as well as typeface, it is necessary to change the font. The VariTyper has a type size range of 3½ to 13 points while the Composer has a range of 7 to 12 points.

C. Leading. Most typewriters have a device which controls the single or double spacing of lines. This device controls the movement of the platen, the cylindrical roller around which the paper is positioned. At the end of each typed line, the carriage is returned to the home or starting position, and the platen automatically advances the paper to make room for the next line. This control of vertical space is much more exact on direct impression machines. The VariTyper has ½ point vertical space increments, from ½ to 18 points, forward and reverse feed. The Composer has 1-point vertical space increments, from 5 to 20 points, as well as 1-point and 4-point manual control of the platen, forward and reverse.

D. Line length. The length of a line composed on a typewriter is controlled by preset margins, and is limited by the length of the paper platen. The direct impression machine uses the same method except that the line length or line measure is calibrated in picas rather than inches.

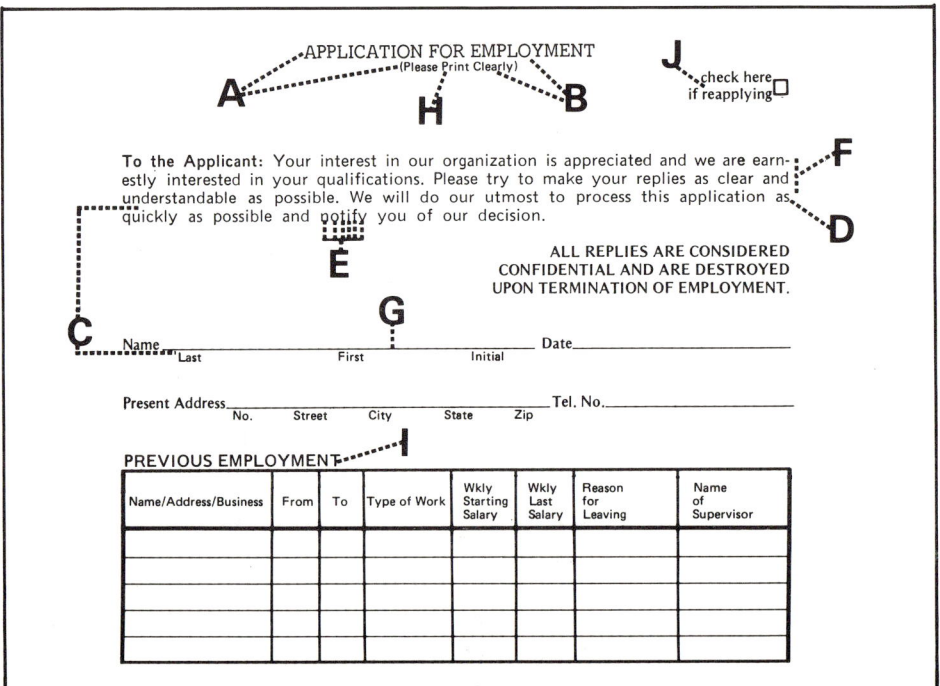

Figure 3. This form produced on the IBM Composer shows many of the possible typographic effects.

Direct Impression Typesetting

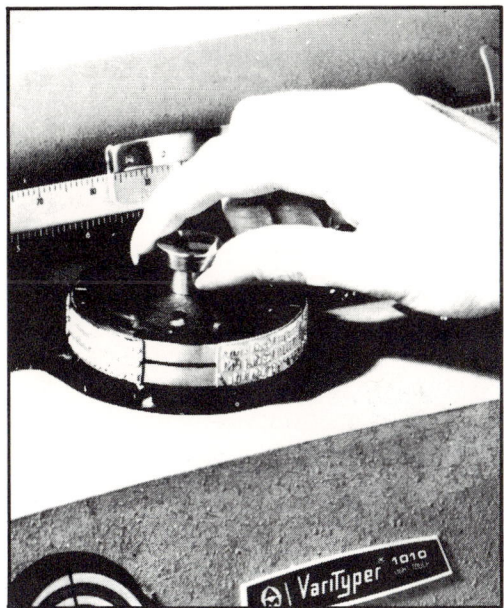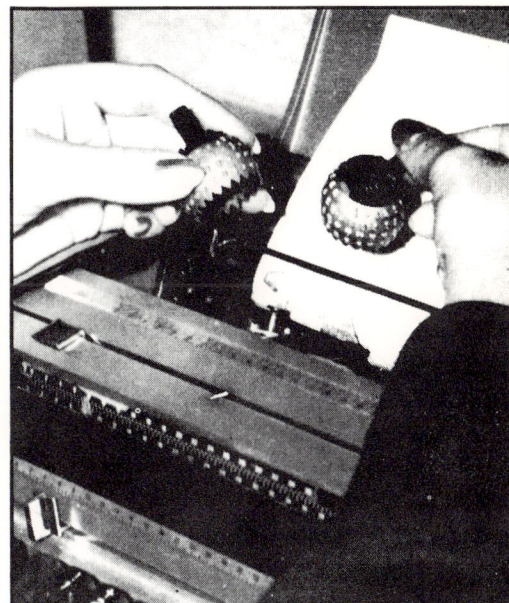

Figure 4. Changing typefaces on the VariTyper (left) and the Composer (right).

E. *Letterspacing.* Perhaps the singlemost unique feature of a direct impression machine from a standard office typewriter is the variable spacing of each character according to its relative width. This control of horizontal spacing is called the escapement. VariTyper has four escapement settings, IBM has three. Escapement varies with the point size being used.

F. *Justification.* Both the VariTyper and the Composer require two typings to achieve justified lines. The first typing determines how much space remains at the end of the line—short of the measure. The second typing inserts the excess space between words to expand the line to full justification.

G. *Rules.* Rules are repeated short-line segments similar to an underscore on a standard typewriter. (See Figure 5.)

H. *Centering.* Both the VariTyper and the Composer require two typings to center words. The first typing is in a non-print mode and is used only to determine the length of the word and its starting point. The second typing is the actual typing of the word(s).

I. *Quad left.* Quad left is the normal positioning of words flush against the left margin.

J. *Quad right.* Quad right requires two typings, the first (non-print) to determine the white space to be located to the left of the composition, and the second typing to compose the words(s).

Understanding Phototypesetting

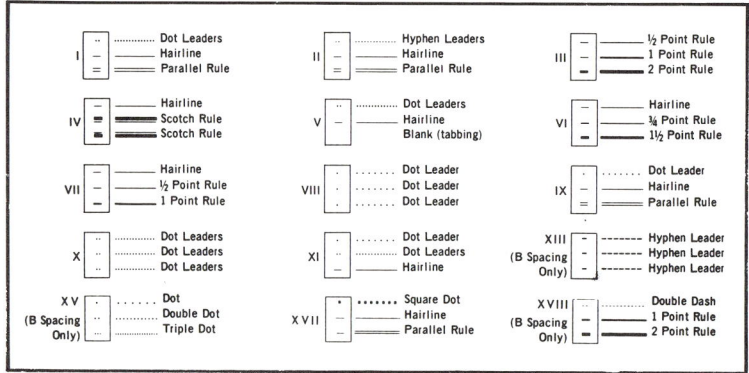

Figure 5. A selection of rules which can be produced on the VariTyper.

Proportional Versus Fixed Spacing

The standard office typewriter uses a fixed spacing system, giving each character, regardless of its horizontal size, the same uniform width. An *i*, for example, the narrowest letter, receives the same space as an *M*, the widest letter. This fixed spacing system is built into the machine and may be either an elite size with twelve characters to the linear inch, or a pica size, with ten characters to the linear inch.

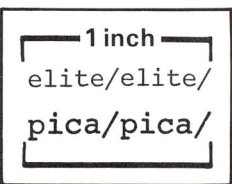

Direct impression machines, on the other hand, are made to simulate typographic composition, and therefore must produce properly letterspaced characters. To achieve this, characters of similar width are grouped together and assigned a relative unit value. For example, the Composer system allots nine units of space to its widest characters, the *m*, *M*, and *W*. The next widest characters, *V*, *X*, *Y*, etc. are given eight units, and so on down to the three unit characters. Table 1 shows the entire unit system.

The VariTyper system assigns its widest characters four units (increments), and its narrowest characters two units. The following table shows relative unit values for all VariTyper fonts.

Escapement, as mentioned previously, is the control of horizontal space. Typewriters have fixed escapement—uniform spacing for each character. Direct impression machines have differential or variable escapements to handle

3 units	4 units	5 units	6 units	7 units	8 units	9 units
i	f	a	b †	B	w	M
j	r	c	d +	C	A	m
l	s	e	h =	E	D	W
.	t	g	k]	F	G	
,	I	v	n 1	L	H	
;	:	z	o 2	T	K	
'	(	J	p 3	Z	N	
-	)	?	q 4		O	
	!	[	u 5		Q	
	/		x 6		R	
			y 7		V	
			P 8		X	
			S 9		Y	
			* 0		&	
					@	
					—	
					¾	
					½	
					¼	

Table 1. *The IBM Composer Unit Value System.*

ROW	2 Increment	3 Increment	4 Increment
L.C.	l i f t j r	a b c d e g h k n	m w
	, . ; -	o p q s u v x y z	
Cap	I	J S	(All capitals except I-J-S)
	, . : !		
Fig		1 2 3 4 5 6 7 8 9 0	% — & ¼ ½ ¾
	, . ' ' ( )	$ ¢ @ # ? * fi fl £ /	

Table 2. *The VariTyper Increment Chart for English fonts.*

different type sizes and/or styles. An *m* on an 8-point IBM type font has a unit value of 9, just as an *m* on a 12-point font. But the 8-point *m* is still physically smaller although it has the same *relative* value. A line of 12-point *m*'s typed in 12-point escapement follows:

mmmmmmmmmmmmmmmmmmmmmmmmm

Compare the letterspacing of the 12-point *m*'s with that of 8-point *m*'s typed in the same escapement.

m m m m m m m m m m m m m m m m m m m m m m m

It appears as though there are spaces between the 8-point *m*'s. The reason for this is that the character unit value, in this example 9, is relative to the escapement. Since the escapement is set for a 12-point font, it moves to the right 9 units of 12-point, rather than 9 units of 8-point.

The Composer has three escapements, color coded red, yellow, and blue.

one pica in red = 12 units
one pica in yellow = 14 units
one pica in blue = 16 units

Each font is color coded according to its size and therefore its relative escapement. In the previous example, the 8-point font (a blue font) was used with a 12-point escapement, which is the red (do not confuse 12 points with 12 units). The *m* has a unit value of 9. Blue fonts have 16 units to the pica. The 8-point *m* therefore, has a relative value of 9/16th when properly spaced. When used with a red escapement, however, the 8-point *m* is spaced 12/16th. The calculation follows:

The machine is set on
red escapement.
An 8-point m is typed.
The machine counts 9 units.
9 units in red = 9/12 = 3/4 pica
3/4 pica of red = 3/4 of 16 units
of an 8-pt. blue font.
3/4 of 16 units = 12/16th.
an m in 8-pt. = 9 units of a
16-unit escapement = 9/16th
12/16 - 9/16 = 3/16 pica of
white space appearing
from use of wrong escapement

The VariTyper system has four escapement values (increment values) labelled A, B, C, and D.

Justification

Direct impression machines can justify lines of type by a technique called spacing out. Spacing out is a method of measuring the space left by lines shorter than the full measure and placing that remaining space between words in the line. This method can be accomplished, by way of illustration, on an ordinary typewriter.

First the copy is typed, with attention to the space remaining at the end of each line.

Then the copy is retyped with the excess space at the end of each line distributed between words to space the line out to fill the measure.

Direct Impression Typesetting

```
This is an example of howx
an ordinary office type-xx
writer can be used to com-
pose justified lines ofxxx
type.

This is an example of  how
an ordinary  office  type-
writer  can  be used to com-
pose  justified  lines  of
type.
```

Direct impression machines use the same idea, but rather than double the spaces between some words, as in the typewriter example, they add small units to word-spaces so that the expanded line is aesthetically and typographically pleasing. As an illustration, suppose that an 18-pica measure is required and the IBM Composer is being used with a red escapement. The normal space between words measures three units, and nine words are typed:

```
You have just learned how to justify copy on
```

The machine scale indicates that the line is five units short of the measure. The unit value of five (along with a color code) is set on a dial and the line is retyped. The machine automatically increases the first five spaces by one unit each, expanding the line by a total of five units to full justification.

```
You have just learned how to justify copy on
```

The Vari-Typer offers models featuring automatic justification. As with the Composer, the rough copy is typed, then the carriage is tabbed to a stop to the right. With the second typing, the necessary space is automatically inserted. The process is repeated for all consecutive lines.

This method of typing both the rough and justified copy on the same line is called parallel justification. A popular alternative is serial justification wherein all the rough copy is typed first, the codes are recorded in the margin, and then all of the lines are retyped in justified form.

Advantages of Direct Impression Typesetting

Setting type by typewriter became a legitimate process in the 1930s, when there was a need for a compatible typesetting device for the office mimeograph. A small printer or in-plant manager could not justify the expense of a Linotype or Monotype, the major typesetting alternatives, and beside that, they really did not suit his needs. Improvements in typewriting devices, including the IBM Executive typewriter featuring proportional character widths, and the Friden Justowriter, with automatic tape-driven justification, helped to secure a place for direct impression typesetting. The VariTyper was one of the first typewriter-like devices specifically made for typesetting purposes. It was in a class by itself until the introduction of the IBM Selectric Composer in 1967.

Direct impression typesetting offers the advantage of visibility, allowing the operator complete control over the placement of characters. This is especially useful in the production of forms, and forms-related work such as organizational charts and sections of brochures and reports.

In early 1975, IBM introduced its Electronic "Selectric" Composer as shown in Figure 6. This desk-top machine features a built-in memory which permits the operator to store, replay, and manipulate up to 8,000 characters at one time. In addition, only one typing is required since mistakes can be corrected by merely writing over the error, and justification, in a number of formats, is automatic.

The introduction of direct entry phototypesetting has eclipsed two advantages long held by direct impression machines, namely, ease of operation and low initial cost. The direct impression machine was sold as the only typesetting machine which a secretary could operate with a minimum of training. Also, being sold for under $5000, there was no phototypesetting device which even came close in price. Today, direct entry phototypesetters compete in price and simplicity, and excel in capability and quality.

Figure 6. The IBM Electronic "Selectric" Composer.

Direct Impression Typesetting

The AM VariTyper, the IBM Composer, and Others

There are many typewriters being used today as cold-type composition machines which do not use variable spacing or single-pass polyethylene ribbons, are not calibrated in picas, and do not have changeable type sizes and styles. These machines are, however, heavy duty office machines designed for providing images suitable for reproduction. The reader should be aware of such machines and be able to evaluate them in relation to a true direct impression typesetter. The following chart compares the VariTyper to the Composer and lists the major functional and design features.

	VariTyper	Composer
Type Selection	1181 including approximately 60 different languages, 3 fraction, and 1 math font	130 including Greek, technical, and math fonts
Font construction	all metal electro formed	electroplated plastic
Characters per font	90	88
Type size range	3½ - 13 points	7 - 12 points
Forms ruling capability	yes	yes
Back space key	1 and 3 increments	1 unit and automatic character back space of last 6 characters
Unit system	4 increments	9 units
Escapements	4 - A, B, C, and D	3 - red, yellow, blue
Power carriage return	yes	yes
Vertical spacing	½ point - 18 points in ½ point increments forward and reverse	5 - 20 point feed in 1 point increments. Manual forward or reverse in 1 or 4 point multiples.
Tab settings	manual, 6 plotting units between columns	automatic, within pica of next column
Impression	electric - keyboard control divided into 10 steps	electric - located on font carrier, divided into 6 steps
Imaging	metal to metal	plated plastic to rubber
Imaging material	polyethylene complete release one pass ribbon	polyethylene complete release one pass ribbon
Justification	automatic	semi-automatic
Justifying procedure	1. Type 2. Tab 3. Type 4. Carriage return	1. Type 2. Read color and number code 3. Set dial 4. Tab 5. Type 6. Carriage return 7. Reset justifying dial
Serial Justification	yes	yes
Models	1010 - standard.... $5335 1360 - engineering machine 24" carriage, unit spacing....$3555	semi-automatic justification selectric.... $4600 automatic justification magnetic tape selectric composer (MT/SC).... $11,340 electronic composer.... $8500

Chart 1. Comparison of the AM VariTyper and the IBM Composer.

4 input devices

Summary

An *input device* is used to convert human readable information, such as an author's manuscript or an advertiser's message, into machine readable codes which can direct the operation of a phototypesetter. The most widely used method of input is the keyboard, which may be a physical part of the typesetter itself, or may be *off-line*.

Some keyboards are capable of determining exactly how many characters of a particular type size and style will fit on one line. Such machines are called *counting* keyboards. Machines which have no means of determining where lines should end are called *non-counting* keyboards. Either counting or non-counting keyboards may have a *visual* display, or may be *blind*.

Keyboards which produce a perforated tape made of plastic, paper, or a sandwich of the two, are called *perforators* or *perforating keyboards*. The punched tape records a series of codes representing characters and machine commands. Other keyboards produce magnetic tape, punched cards, or typewritten pages of machine readable English.

The process of writing machine instructions for line length, point size, typeface, etc. is called *mark-up*. Mark-up determines what the finished job will look like, and therefore, requires care and planning.

Trade Terms

alignment - positioning of characters on a common baseline.

bit - a data hole or perforation in paper or mylar tape, or a single recorded electrical charge on magnetic tape used to signify character codes.

blind keyboard - a keyboard which has no visual indicators.

counting keyboard - a keyboard capable of subtracting the unit width of each character typed from the overall line measure.

CRT (Cathode-Ray Tube) - a TV-type tube used as a line display on some input keyboards.

direct entry - a method of phototypesetting wherein the keyboard is an integrated part of the typesetter itself.

discretionary hyphen - a code placed between syllables of words usually incorrectly hyphenated by typesetting machines.

end-of-line decision - the point at which the keyboard operator determines that there are enough characters in the line to fill the measure.

face value - a measurement, in points, of the cap height of the typeface. This is usually equivalent to 2/3 of the point size.

fan fold - a length of paper tape which has been accordion folded in six inch sections.

floating display - a keyboard mounted display upon which typed characters electronically appear.

format - a) relating to the style of design of a printed piece including its typeface(s), page size, cover etc., b) the prescribed manner in which typographic elements are handled. A keyboard format key has memory locations in which such instructions may be stored.

hard copy - a typewritten proof of perforated or magnetic tape used by a keyboard operator to spot errors before he continues to the next line.

hardware - a computer term referring to equipment as opposed to software which refers to computer programs.

hard wire - an electrical connection between two machines.

hot zone - the justification area at the end of a line.

hyphenless justification - lines justified by variable word and letterspacing rather than by breaking words.

input - a device for entering data for machine processing.

Input Revision Typewriter (IRT) - a typewriter with a magnetic recording device.

interface - a device which facilitates communication between two or more different machines.

interlock - a keyboard option found on some older keyboards which prevents more than one key being struck at one time. Modern keyboards use a buffer to store the additional keystrokes until the input recording device can catch up with the operator.

justified tape - perforated or magnetic tape with complete end-of-line information.

keyboard layout - an arrangement of alphanumeric and function keys to suit a particular purpose.

mark-up - the process of determining the phototypesetter function codes and numeric descriptors which will translate manuscript copy into typeset galleys.

mixing - the use of more than one size or style of typeface on a single line.

mnemonic - a letter or group of letters used as a memory aid, i.e. a formula or code.

mylar - a plastic or plastic and paper laminate tape used for perforating purposes.

non-counting keyboard - a keyboard which is not capable of counting character unit widths.

OCR (Optical Character Recognition) - a machine which is capable of translating human readable copy into machine (phototypesetter) readable codes.

off-line - a device which is not wired into a system.

output - the result of a process.

overset - a line which exceeds the measure.

perforator - a keyboard device which produces a punched tape.

precedence codes - a code which changes the meaning of the code or codes which follow.

recording medium - a means of retaining magnetic impulses (magnetic tape) or data holes (perforated tape) for future use.

rub out - to erase, delete, or kill information on a magnetic or perforated tape.

running tape - perforated or magnetic tape with no end-of-line information. Sometimes called idiot tape.

secretarial shift - a single key on a perforating keyboard which when depressed will cause all succeeding characters to be in shift position. Releasing the key returns the board to the unshift position.

splice - the point at which two lengths of tape are joined together by an adhesive.

sprocket - the feed holes in perforated tape.

strip - a two to four foot section of perforated tape.

super shift - a precedence code used to access characters or functions not found on a keyboard. See precedence codes.

take - a length of processed tape for a single job.

TTS code (Teletypesetter) - a six level tape coding system.

TTS shift - a keyboard arrangement with one key for shift and another for unshift.

unjustified tape - a tape with no end-of-line information. See running tape.

visual display - either a built-in or optional keyboard accessory which provides an electronic representation of keyboarded characters to the operator.

width plug - a magazine with character width values for a specific typeface or group of typefaces which is plugged into a counting keyboard.

word processing - use of a recording device to revise typewritten copy.

Introduction

The International Typographic Composition Association's Committee on Computer Terminology defines input as "the device or collective set of devices used for bringing data into another device." In other words, an input device is an interface between man and machine, a means of translating readable codes. Most automated typesetting systems depend upon a keyboard to produce a recording medium (perforated tape, magnetic tape, etc.) which can direct the operation of a typesetting device.

Keyboards

Keyboards were direct developments of early attempts to mechanize the manual process of setting type. The first keyboard machine is generally credited to Dr. William Church of Vermont in 1822 (see Figure 1). The Church machine was commercially unsuccessful, as were those of many of his colleagues. By the end of the nineteenth century, however, two typesetting machines had clearly demonstrated their usefulness: the Linotype and the Monotype. From a keyboard standpoint, these two machines represent two configurations which are still used today. The Linotype has the keyboard built into the machine itself and is, therefore, classified as a direct entry machine. It operates in real time; each stroke of a key immediately results in the composing of a character. The Monotype system, on the other hand, has a separate keyboard and caster. The keyboard is off-line and produces a perforated paper ribbon which can be used to control the caster. In this configuration the caster is not limited to the speed of the operator. It can cast type as quickly as it can "read" the holes in the paper ribbon. Another clear advantage is that many keyboard operators can prepare ribbons to feed to one caster.

In 1926, Walter Morey proposed a method of operating linecasting machines (Linotype and Intertype) in much the same way as Monotype machines, and from distant locations. His idea made use of existing keyboard perforators used for wire communication purposes. Within a year, the newly formed Teletype Corporation had a trial installation of the Teletypesetter System (TTS) in Chicago. The war interrupted production, but by 1951 the company had over 400 systems in operation.

Figure 1. The Church machine, generally regarded as the first mechanical typesetting machine.

Keyboard Classification

Today, keyboards are generally off-line, that is, not hard wired to the typesetter itself. Typesetters which do have the keyboard integrated, or hard wired, are classified as direct entry machines. In addition to these two major divisions, there are four important characteristics of keyboards which are always used to describe their input operation:

Counting. A keyboard is classified as a counting board (keyboard) if it is capable of subtracting the width of each keyed character from the overall line measure. Systems vary, but usually when there is less than 3 ems of space left at the end of the line, there is a visual and/or audible signal indicating the justification range or hot zone. The line must be ended with a return code (like returning the carriage on a typewriter to begin a new line) before the counting mechanism reaches zero, or an overset situation will occur. An overset line is one with more characters than space, and usually results, if it gets that far, in a stalled typesetter. The operator makes an end-of-line decision on where within the justification range the line will stop or break (hyphenate). The output or product of a counting board is a justified tape having exactly the right number of characters in each line to completely fill the measure.

The Monotype keyboard was the first successful counting mechanism for the composition of justified lines. Since character widths sometimes varied from one font to the next, the Monotype used changeable justifying scales to compensate. (See Figure 2.) The Teletypesetter (TTS) keyboards made use of changeable width plugs, with unit values for specific typefaces wired in. (See Figure 3.) Another method of character width storage is the printed circuit (PC) board. PC boards can carry width information for many different typefaces, and are easily changed. A more sophisticated method of storing character width information is by computer memory storage. Keyboards equipped with memory can be programmed with a width tape to store up to thirty-two or more different fonts.

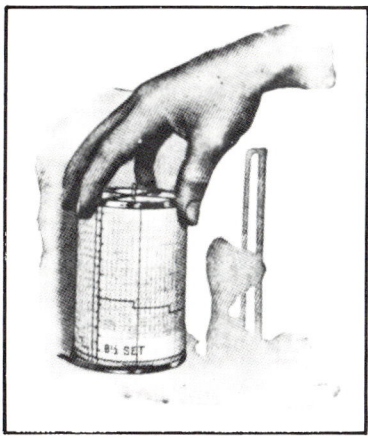

Figure 2. The Monotype justifying scale is changed each time there is a change in the set width of a typeface.

Understanding Phototypesetting

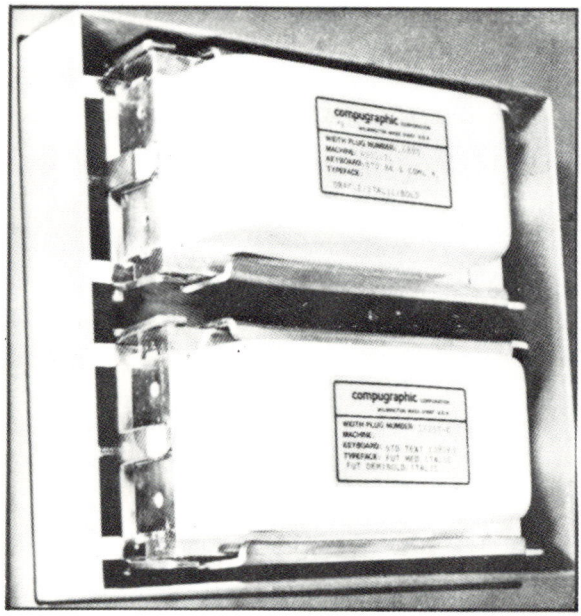

Figure 3. The Compugraphic CompuWriter series for direct entry keyboards use width plugs to store character width information.

Non-counting. Keyboards which do not have the capability of determining the unit value of each keyed character are classified as non-counting boards. The output of these machines is endless (except for end of paragraph codes) non-justified (idiot) tape. End-of-line decisions, or justification and hyphenation (H and J), are accomplished later in the production cycle, either by computer or the phototypesetter itself.° Most counting keyboards can be used in a non-counting mode.

Blind. Keyboards which do not provide any visual indication as to what has been keyed-in are classified as blind machines. There are both counting and non-counting blind keyboards.

Visual. Keyboards which allow the operator to examine the characters and codes which are being composed are classified as visual. There are currently six kinds of visual indicators available:

last character - keyboard panel displays the last character or function codes entered.

last code - keyboard panel displays the bit locations of the last character or function code entered. (See Figure 4.)

hardcopy - the keyboard utilizes a typewriter mechanism which produces a typed copy of each character and function code entered.

°*Some systems are capable of hyphenless justification, wherein space is added or subtracted from between words and/or letters rather than carrying parts of words over to the next line.*

Input Devices

floating display - characters and function codes move across a one line electronic display. (See Figure 4.)

CRT (cathode-ray rube) - characters and function codes appear on a TV-type screen. The operator has the ability to edit the copy before it leaves the screen and is recorded on the output medium.

Keyboards are either counting or non-counting, or both, blind or visual, or both.° There are counting blind boards, non-counting blind boards, counting visual boards, and non-counting visual boards.

Figure 4. *The Harris TxT UJ-6 Perforator is a non-counting visual board with both floating 16-character and last code displays.*

° *A visual machine can be made blind by covering the display. The advantage of a blind machine is that it is less of a distraction to the operator.*

Keyboard Options

Keyboards are bought to meet the specific needs of the user. Some of the things to be considered when choosing a board are:

>The phototypesetter it will drive.
>The type of work (straight matter, advertisements, tabular matter, etc.) to be set.
>Number and location of keys on the board (one to access each character in the font).
>Number of function (command) keys.
>Visual display(s).
>Justified or unjustified output.

In addition, there are a number of standard and optional features which simplify the setting of complex composition. Figure 5 shows a fairly typical keyboard layout, an explanation of some of these keys, as well as others, follows:

Figure 5. The Harris TxT UJ-6 Perforator keyboard, like most layouts, has contrasting colored alphanumeric and command keys.

>*Format* - a key which can be programmed with a "string" of frequently used codes or alphanumerics.
>
>*Reverse Tape Feed* - backs tape so that a code or codes can be deleted or rubbed out.
>
>*Rub out* - places perforations in all channels of a frame. May be used to eliminate a single character or code, a word, or an entire line. Also labelled as "delete," "kill," or "erase," a character, word or line.
>
>*Tape Feed* - forwards tape and punches feed holes. Used at the beginning of tapes to make a "leader" for labelling, and to facilitate threading the phototypesetter reader.
>
>*Shift* - "secretary shift" - when depressed characters which follow are in shift position until the key is raised (single key). "TTS shift" - shift key places font in shift position until unshift key is depressed (two keys).
>
>*Super shift (SS)* - a precedence code, that is, a code which precedes a series of commands or characters, which alerts the phototypesetter to a change in function, or to locate a pi character.

Input Devices

Stop - a code which signals the phototypesetter reader to stop.

Discretionary hyphen (disc. hyp.) - used in unjustified tape between syllables of words which could be improperly hyphenated by computer logic. If such a word does need to be hyphenated, it is broken at a discretionary hyphen location.

Keyboard Output

Most keyboards used in phototypesetting systems produce a punched paper tape. Such machines are called perforators or perforating keyboards, and the tapes which they produce are based upon the TTS code configuration. The TTS system uses a 6 level tape, coding each character or command by the presence or absence of holes along the 6 channels. Figure 6 shows a piece of TTS tape with the 6 possible data holes (bits) or perforations.

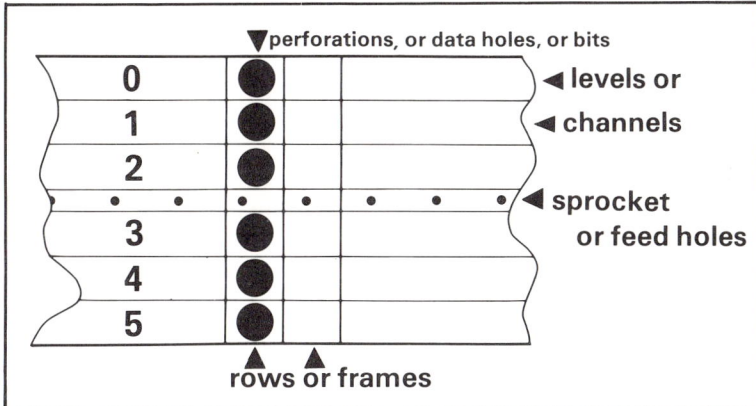

Figure 6. The parts of a six-level TTS perforated tape.

The Coding System

The concept of perforated tape coding is quite simple. Combinations of perforations can be used to represent a number of alphanumerics or machine instructions—that number is limited by the number of channels in the tape. Consider a tape which has two channels. The presence of a hole can be represented by a "1," the absence by a "0." With two levels there are four possible codes.

    00
    01
    10
    11

With three levels there are eight possibilities:

000
001
011
010
100
101
110
111

With five there are 32, and with six there are 64 possible bit arrangements.

Precedence Codes

Font sizes vary from one phototypesetter manufacturer to another, and their arrangements and contents vary according to their intended use. An average typographic font has about 100 characters; this is not surprising when one considers that a standard office typewriter has 88 or more. The 64 unique TTS code combinations can be expanded to twice that size° in the same way that a 44 key typewriter can type 88 characters—by the use of precedence codes. A precedence code is one which identifies the following code as having a different meaning. Just as the shift key on a typewriter precedes a small *a* and results in a cap *A*, doubling the utility of the single key, the shift key on a typesetting keyboard has the same effect.

Both shift and unshift are considered precedence codes, as is a third code called red ribbon shift, control case shift, or more commonly, super shift (SS). Super shift codes are especially useful in entering control codes from keyboards with few or no control keys. For example, to enter a line measure of 24 picas from a board with a line measure control key, the operator would depress the line measure key and (usually) four digits, 2400 (24 picas, 00 points). To enter the same information from a board with no line measure control key the operator would key in:

SS/SM2400/SS

SM is a mnemonic, a means of helping the operator remember the function which it is to fulfill, namely setting the measure. Table 1 shows a list of mnemonics used with super shift codes to access control functions.

°*Some codes such as rub out, tape fed, elevate, return, and fixed spaces are the same in shift and unshift conditions.*

Table 1. Mnemonics used with Super Shift Precedence Code (Compugraphic 9000)

Function	Mnemonics
½-point line space	SS H P
1 point line space	SS O P
line space	SS L S
insert space	SS L S
insert leader	SS I L
insert rule	SS I R
line measure set	SS S M
line space set	SS S L
tab set	SS S T
auto tab	SS A T
tab	SS T B
char. comp. set	SS S C
no flash	SS S O
space off	SS S X
flash only	SS O F
manual line ending	SS M E
auto line ending	SS A E
auto character comp	SS A C
variable char. comp	SS V C
letterspace, on	SS L J
letterspace off	SS J X
hyphenation, on	SS H O
hyphenation, off	SS H X
forward 1 unit	SS A U
back 1 unit	SS S U
forward 1 point	SS A P
back 1 point	SS S P
carriage reset	SS C R
end line	SS E L

Reading Paper Tape

The TTS code can be expanded to include more code combinations by the addition of two more levels or channels. This 8-level tape, originally used in data processing systems, is used as a recording medium for phototypesetting computer programs and for operating sophisticated typesetting systems with large character sets (fonts) and intricate styles of composition. Many phototypesetting machines are capable of accepting both 6- and 8-level tape.

It is to the advantage of every perforator operator to learn how to read paper tape. Figure 7 shows the TTS codes.

Phototypesetting readers which optically sense the presence or absence of perforations, generally accept either *center feed*, or *advance feed* tape. Center feed tape has the sprocket or feed holes located in line with the data holes as shown here:

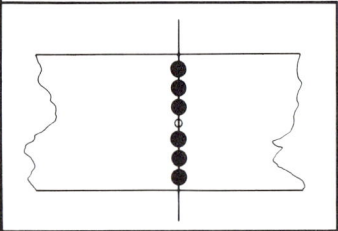

Advance feed tapes, on the other hand, have the feed holes aligned with the leading edge of the data holes:

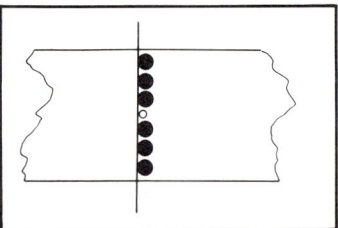

Other technical information related to paper tape is shown in Table 2.

	6 level	8 level
width	7/8"	1"
sprocket hole diameter	.046"	.046"
data hole diameter	.072"	.072"
character density	10 char./in.	10 char./in.
sprocket location	center	below center
usual length of roll	1000'	1000'
tape thickness	2½ - 4 mils	2½ - 4 mils

Table 2. Table Information Regarding Paper Tape

Input Devices

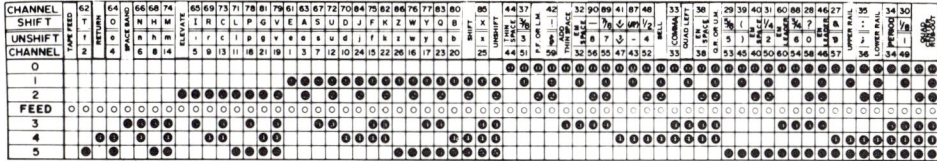

Figure 7. The TTS code structure.

Magnetic Tape

Magnetic tape or mag tape has become a popular alternative to paper tape. Although mag tape has long been used in data processing, it is from the home entertainment field which the typesetting equipment manufacturers borrowed the magnetic cassette. Cassettes are small, easy to handle, self-enclosed reels of oxide coated 1/8" tape.

Like paper tape, magnetic tape records character codes as patterns of bits. The bits, usually 8, are represented by changes in the polarity of the magnetic field. To accomplish this, the tape is brought in contact with a parallel series of *write heads* (electromagnets), one for each track or level. The character to be recorded is represented as positive and negative charges along the write heads. These charges are magnetically recorded on the tape.

Other Recording Media

Card Comp is an interface system marketed by CompuSystems of Lombard, Illinois.° An interface is a device which facilitates communication between two machines. Paper tape produced on any perforator can be fed into the Card Comp Keyboard Interpreter Unit to produce punched 80 column computer cards. (See Figure 8.) A stack or deck of these cards is then placed in the Card Comp Typesetter Interface Unit which is connected directly to the typesetter's control logic. The cards are read as

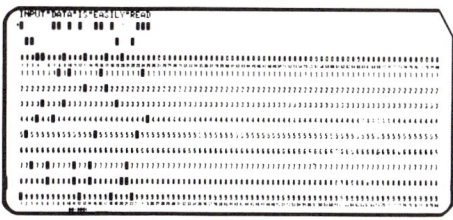

Figure 8. Punched cards are discrete units of information which can be easily updated.

°Also known as the Race II system by Warlock Computer Corporation of Georgetown, Connecticut.

quickly as tape. Unlike tape, however, which is a continuous stream of machine-readable codes, the cards are human-readable. Also, corrections, changes and additions are easily made by removing or inserting cards.

Tape produced on the IBM MT/ST direct impression typesetter can also be used to drive a phototypesetter, with the use of an interface made by Digi-Data Corporation. The system can be used on or off line.

One of the fastest methods of input to a typesetter is by OCR, optical character recognition. OCR machines simulate both the operation of the human eye, by electronically interpreting human readable characters, and the operation of a perforator keyboard by producing a punched tape.° Ordinary office typewriters (usually IBM Selectrics) with special OCR fonts (see Figure 9) produce double or triple spaced (to leave room for editorial changes) typewritten sheets which can be scanned by the OCR machine. (See Figure 10.) The advantage is not only the tremendous speed by which the OCR machine can scan pages of text (as fast as 500 cps and faster), but also the fact that the original copy or manuscript, if neat and properly prepared, can be used as the input. This method of avoiding the retyping of copy is called *capturing keystrokes* and is also the basis of another system called word processing.

```
BAR CODE ADVANTAGES:

    Lowest Cost

    Less Maintenance

    Design Simplicity

    Portable

    Reliability

    Low Error Rate

    Parity Check
```

Figure 9. The Datatype OCR system uses bar codes beneath alphanumerics for machine interpretation. Other OCR systems use alphanumerics which the optical readers can interpret directly.

° *A mag tape may also be produced, or the OCR may be hard wired directly to the typesetter, or to a computer for H and J.*

Input Devices

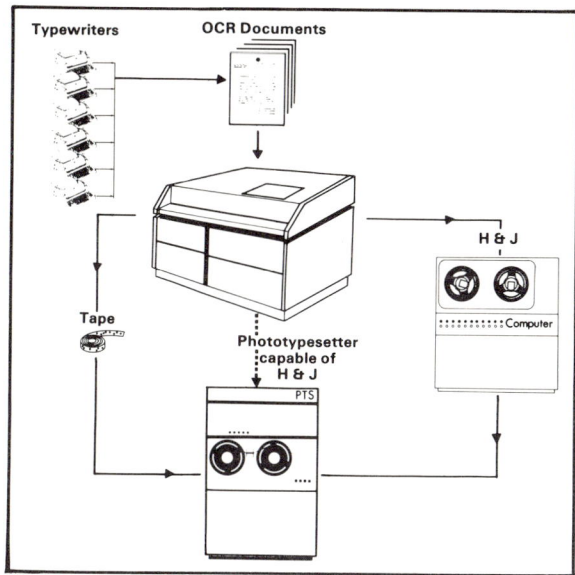

Figure 10. An OCR machine is an interface device which translates human-readable language into machine-usable codes.

Word Processing

Word processing originated in the business world to handle high volume, repetitive material which was subject to change, editing or revision. The first machine capable of these functions was the IBM MT/ST system, a direct impression typesetting machine with mag tape input/output (I/O). The MT/ST, like other Input Revision Typewriters (IRT), is capable of recording, or capturing, each operator keystroke on an output medium, usually mag tape or card. The output medium can be played back, like a tape recorder, and edited. If revisions are necessary, the operator types them in at the appropriate locations and the recording medium is likewise changed. Using the proper interface devices, such as those made by Redactron, it is possible to drive a phototypesetter with the output from an IRT.

Keyboard Layout

With the exception of the alpha characters, practically every keyboard layout is arranged differently. Anyone who has used more than one typewriter knows that it is always necessary to check for the location of the back space key and margin release key as well as to note, among other things, if the board has a number 1, or if the lower case l must be used. Most keyboards used for typesetting not only have more keys for accessing alphanumeric characters, but also additional keys for entering machine commands. A number of layouts are shown in Figure 11.

Understanding Phototypesetting

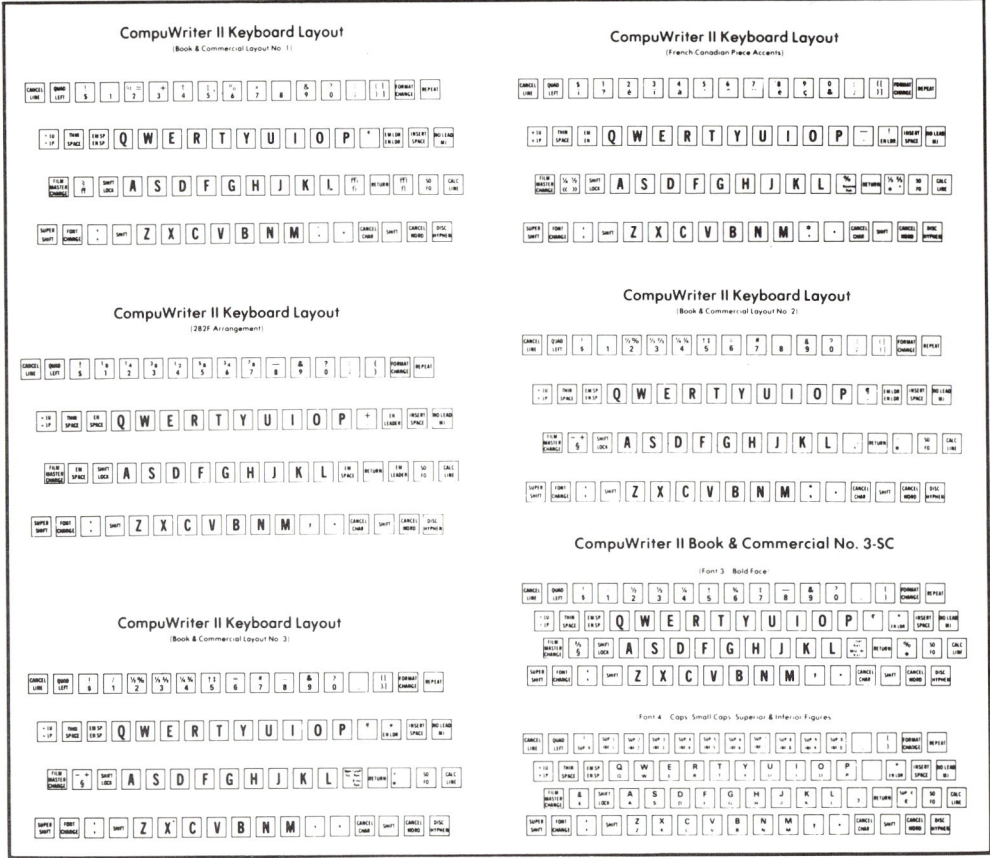

Figure 11. Keyboard layouts vary not only from one keyboard to the next, but also according to the final purpose of the composition. Here are some of the layouts available on the CompuWriter II direct entry phototypesetter.

Direct Keyboarding

When a keyboard is physically a part of the phototypesetter, the operator is able to directly enter input information without the use of a recording medium. (See Figure 12.) The major disadvantage of this system is that the speed of the machine is "operator determined," which in all cases limits the productivity.

The VariTyper Comp/Set 500 shown in Figure 13 is a direct entry phototypesetter with many features found on larger, more expensive machines. The type disc is unique in that it carries the character width information on its face, thus eliminating width tapes, cards or plugs. The operator inputs at a CRT keyboard having visual control over all the typographic parameters as well as the alphanumeric input. In addition, the operator can make unlimited corrections on the line being keyboarded, assuring that the line which is sent to the photo unit is free of error.

Input Devices

Figure 12. The CompuWriter Jr. is a self-contained keyboard and phototypesetting photo unit.

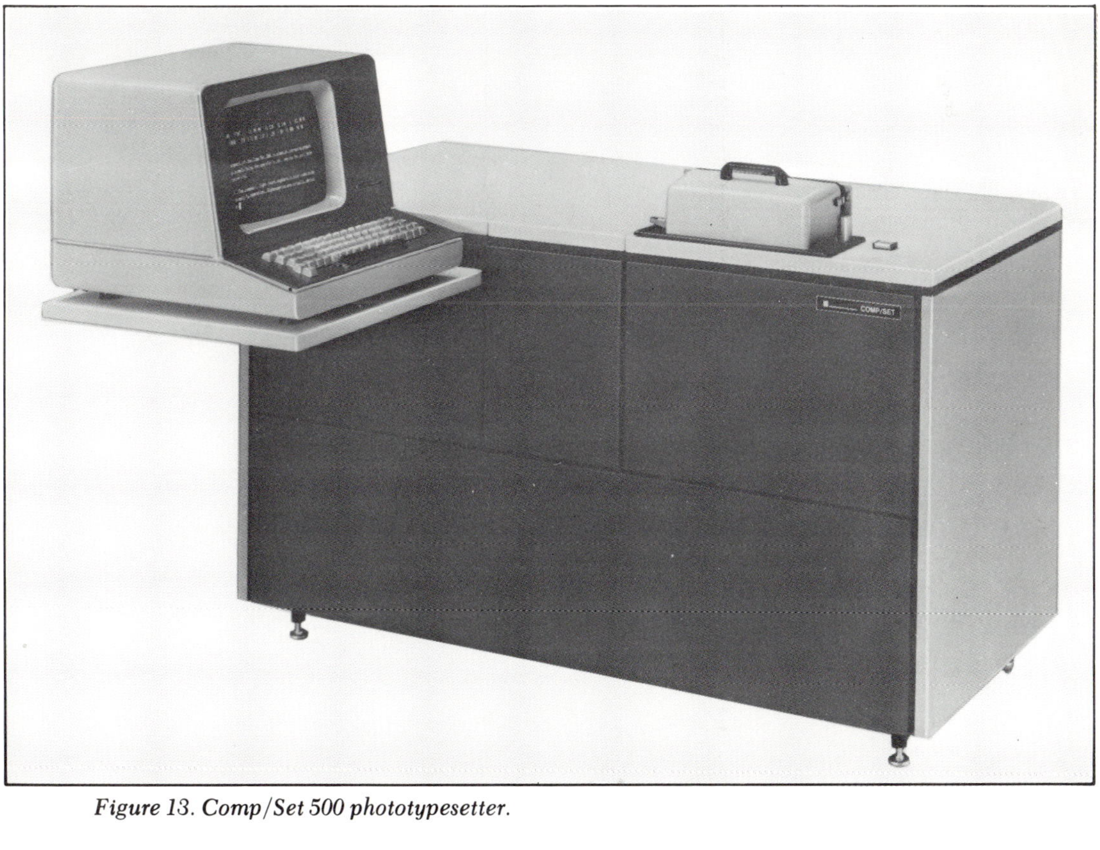

Figure 13. Comp/Set 500 phototypesetter.

Mark-up

Mark-up is the process of specifying machine function codes for the proper operation of the phototypesetter. These codes are a means of describing to the typesetter (operator and machine) how long the measure should be, which typeface(s) should be used, how much space should be placed between lines, and much more.

The mnemonics and abbreviations used to mark copy vary widely, but regardless of how they are noted, they always describe the same functions. The line measure, for example, is always specified in points and picas, and may be indicated by a capital X. A 24-pica measure would be marked:

X24

If the keyboard does not have a line measure key, the command would require further specification, such as:

CC24.0

as used on the Singer Photomix 8400 and the Graphic Systems 1 to signify a change in column width.

A typeface may be marked by its English name, or by its font number location in the phototypesetter. Optima, for example, may be in the third font position and may be marked in English as:

Opt.

or mnemonically as:

f3

standing for "font" or "face" number 3. Type size may be written between parenthesis:

(24)

or as:

24 pt.; p24; CP24

depending upon the system.

The key to mark-up, however, is in specifying leading. Leading is the white space between lines of type, and it is achieved in phototypesetting systems by advancing the photographic material (paper or film).

In most applications, the film advance, or leading, is measured from the baseline of the characters in one line to the baseline of characters in the next.

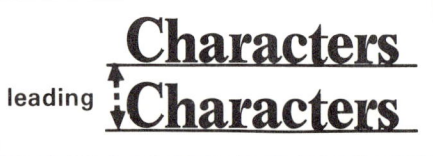

The capitals, figures, and lower case ascenders all rest on the baseline, the descenders dip below. The cap height usually represents the face value of the typeface, and the face value generally measures 2/3 of the point size.

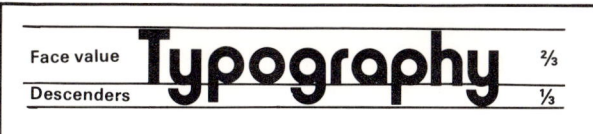

The face value is an important consideration in phototypesetting, especially in advertising work. Consider this ad:

First the "Sweetheart" is set in 12-point caps:

The word soap is set in 48-point caps, with a face value of 32 points. The 32 points is the minimum possible line spacing, since any film advance short of 32 would result in lines being set over one another:

The final line has both 10-point and 72-point type sizes, both resting on the same baseline. The film is advanced 9 points to accommodate the 10-point type (plus a slight space); the 72-point type is set at the same time, quad right.

When lines of upper and lower case characters are set, a leading allowance must be made for the descenders. This allowance is the remaining 1/3 of the type size plus any additional points or half points. The example which follows shows samples of text set at various line space values.

Set at Face Value

The parameters are initial codes which are used to program the phototypesetting machine for a particular job. The parameters always include the line measure, line spacing, type size, and typeface. Parameters may also include tabs, character compensation, and the options of automatic or manual line ending, variable or automatic character compensation, justification by letterspacing, and hyphenation program on or off.

8 pt. type set at face value (6 pt.)

Set at Point Size

The parameters are initial codes which are used to program the phototypesetting machine for a particular job. The parameters always include the line measure, line spacing, type size, and typeface. Parameters may also include tabs, character compensation, and the options of automatic or manual line ending, variable or automatic character compensation, justification by letterspacing, and hyphenation program on or off.

8 pt. type set at the pt. size

Point Size plus ½ point

The parameters are initial codes which are used to program the phototypesetting machine for a particular job. The parameters always include the line measure, line spacing, type size, and typeface. Parameters may also include tabs, character compensation, and the options of automatic or manual line ending, variable or automatic character compensation, justification by letterspacing, and hyphenation program on or off.

8 pt. type set at the pt. size + ½ pt.

Point Size plus 1 point

The parameters are initial codes which are used to program the phototypesetting machine for a particular job. The parameters always include the line measure, line spacing, type size, and typeface. Parameters may also include tabs, character compensation, and the options of automatic or manual line ending, variable or automatic character compensation, justification by letterspacing, and hyphenation program on or off.

8 pt. type set at the pt. size + 1 pt.

Leading is usually indicated by a slash (/), or horizontal rule (—). It is sometimes marked in this way to show the point size and the leading. For example,

10/12 or $\frac{10}{12}$

refers to a 10-point type with 12 points of line spacing (2 points of leading). Some mark-up systems use the slash to indicate leading only, such as

12/

or as a means of indicating two leading values, referring to two blocks of copy.

12/18

Input Devices

```
   :xxxxxxxxxxxxxxxxxxxxxxxx
12 :xxxxxxxxxxxxxxxxxxxxxxxx   10/12
   :xxxxxxxxxxxxxxxxxxxxxxxx
18 :xxxxxxxxxxxxxxxxxxxxxxxx
    xxxxxxxxxxxxxxxxxxxxxxxx
    xxxxxxxxxxxxxxxxxxxxxxxx   10/12
    xxxxxxxxxxxxxxxxxxxxxxxx
    xxxxxxxxxxxxxxxxxxxxxxxx
```

```
Taking a Trip?

-picture-

Protect your money by carrying
American Impress Traveler's Checks

Better than money, because if they're
lost or stolen, we'll replace them for
the same price you paid - with no
cost for all the extra bother.


Accepted Worldwide, and why not?

-logo-

The American Impress Traveler's Check Co.
```

Figure 14. The typewritten copy.

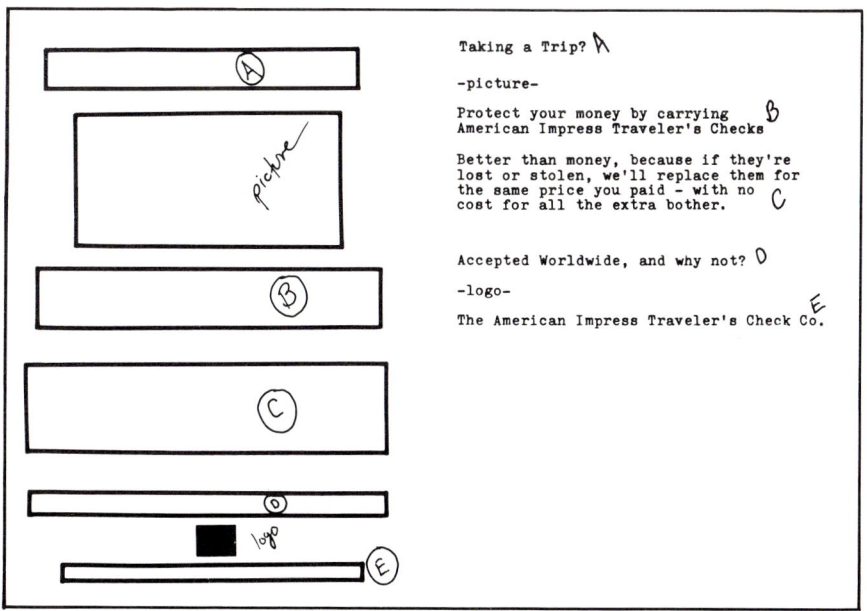

Figure 15. The rough layout, keyed to the copy by letters identifying each block.

79

Understanding Phototypesetting

Figure 14 shows a typewritten ad which is to be marked-up for typesetting. The mark-up man first determines the printed area within which the copy must fit (copyfitting), and if an artist or someone else has not already designed a layout he may do so (Figure 15). The copy is then marked with all appropriate codes needed to produce the desired effect (Figure 16). The machine or keyboard operator enters the mark-up information to produce the finished composition (Figure 17).

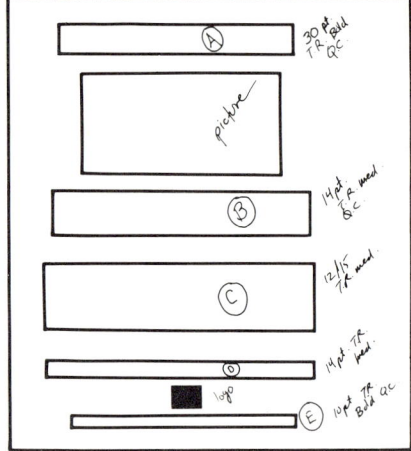

Figure 16. The copy marked up for typesetting.

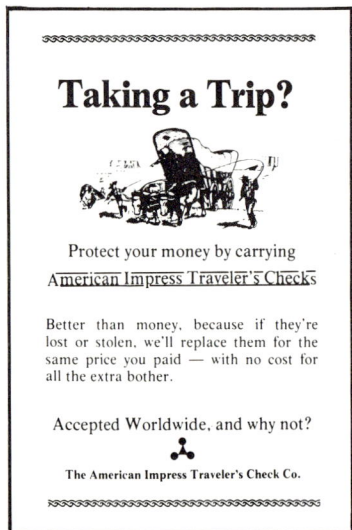

Figure 17. The completed composition.

The Way It Was

Accounts differ as to the form and origin of the earliest type characters, but it is known that entire pages of characters were carved in wooden blocks as early as 400 A.D. by the Chinese. The blocks were inked and pressed against paper in much the same way that linoleum block prints are made today.

The Chinese are also credited with the invention of individual type characters formed of hardened clay and assembled or "typeset." About two hundred years later in the mid-1200s, the Koreans cast type out of bronze and a book was actually printed from such type in 1397 A.D.

In about 1440 A.D. in Mainz, Germany, Johann Gutenberg (see Figure 1) brought together many previously existing inventions and merged them into one of the earliest printing systems. His accomplishments consist of the accurate casting of type, in large quantities, from brass molds and the subsequent union of his types with the inventions of his predecessors. His contribution is not to be minimized, however, for he made the production of books and the notion of mass communication possible.

Figure 1. Thorwaldsen's statue of John Gutenberg.

Understanding Phototypesetting

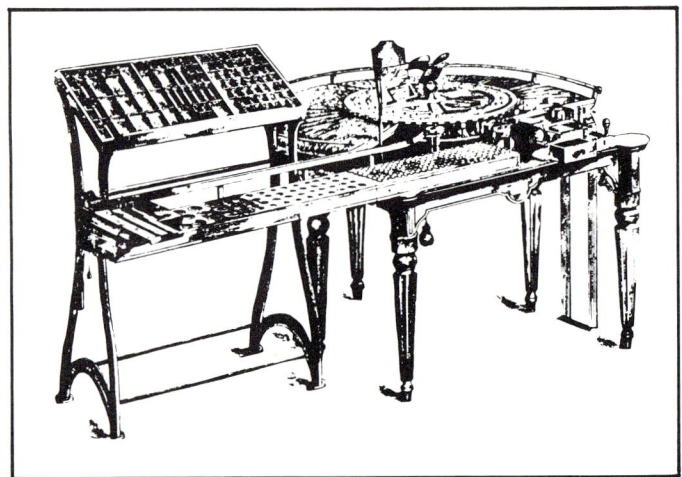

Figure 2. The Alden typesetter and distributor.

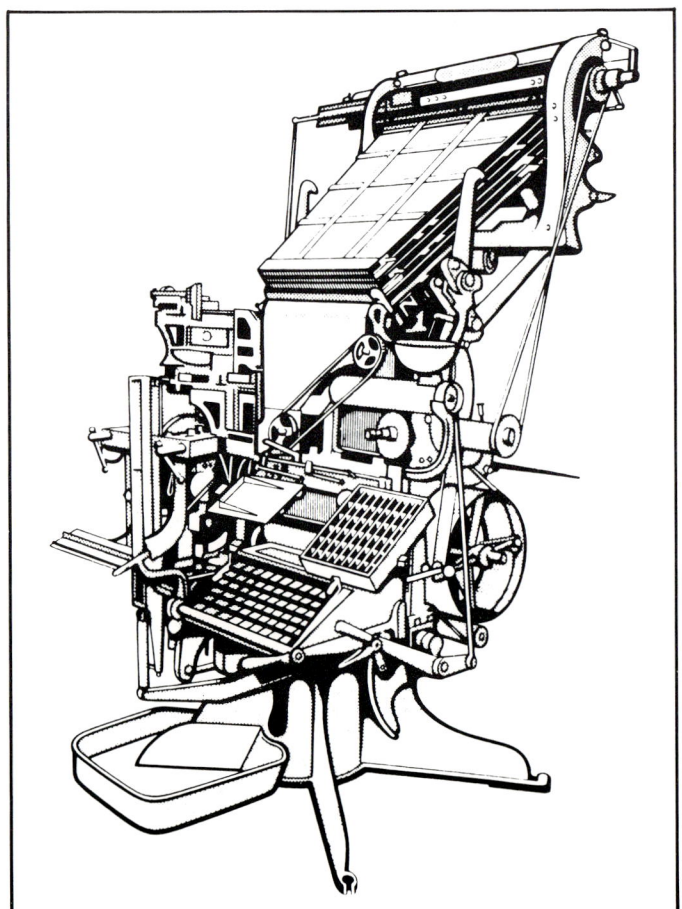

Figure 3. The Linotype—circa 1950.

The casting and composition of type by hand remained a manual process until the mid-nineteenth century when a transitional or developmental stage began. During this period of industrial revolution, there were many attempts at automating hand composition by using machines to assemble pre-cast type characters. Most attempts were unsuccessful. (See Figure 2.)

In the late nineteenth century the Linotype (see Figure 3) and Monotype machines were developed. Unlike previous typesetting machines which merely assembled pre-cast type characters, the Linotype and Monotype composed character matrices and cast solid lines (Linotype) or single characters (Monotype). These machines are also significant in that they represent two production configurations still in use today, namely direct keyboarding (Linotype) and off-line keyboarding (Monotype). As will be seen in Chapter 6, first-generation phototypesetters are direct descendents of these two machines.

5 editing devices

Summary

Locating and correcting errors is an ever-present problem in phototypesetting. Error elimination begins with *editing* copy before it is keyboarded, then either *proofreading* the keyboard output before the type is set, or proofreading the typeset galleys afterward.

One method of error detection is the location of errors prior to the actual typesetting. A computer can be used to process information on an unjustified tape and produce a proof on a high speed line printer. A more popular and less costly method is the use of a *Visual Display Terminal (VDT)*. A VDT is a keyboard with a CRT which can be used to display and edit OCR, or perforated or magnetic tape input.

Other methods of locating errors before type is set include matrix proofers, hard copy keyboards and visual displays, and composition and make-up terminals.

Editing Devices

Trade Terms

AA's (Author's Alterations) - changes made to a typeset galley by its author. As these changes are to be expected, printers usually allow authors about 15% of the total composition cost for corrections. Corrections which exceed this allowance are charged against the author's royalty account.

CAM (Composition and Make-up terminal) - a CRT display device capable of showing and changing exact point sizes and character widths. The closest electronic simulation of typeset material available.

clean tape - a tape free of errors.

controller - a computer device which directs the operation of multiple on-line terminals.

copy reading - a method of proofreading requiring two people, one to read aloud, the other to follow on the typeset galley proof.

cursor - a placemarker on a VDT screen taking the form of a flickering square of light or a character underline.

editing - the process of directing the style and content of a publication.

matrix proofer - a device which prints lines of electrostatically generated characters at high speed. Used as a method of proofreading.

monospace - the fixed unit spacing system used on the screen of a VDT.

proofs - reproductions of material which has been typeset. Proofs are used to locate errors and to indicate changes.

proofreading - the process of reading and marking or correcting copy before or after it is typeset.

scrolling - the process of moving lines out of computer memory and across the face of a VDT display screen.

transposition - a keyboarding error involving the improper positioning of adjacent characters or words.

VDT (Visual Display Terminal) - a device used to edit and correct input media before typesetting. Also Video Display Terminal and Visual Display Tube.

Introduction

Typesetting errors are a fact of life. They slip into perforated tape and other forms of input in an almost systematic way. Errors may take the form of omitted letters, words, or entire blocks, as well as misinterpretation of the manuscript and transposed letters or sections of copy.

Understanding Phototypesetting

Finding and correcting errors is one of the most expensive and time consuming aspects of phototypesetting. The process usually begins with some form of editing of the original manuscript or copy to eliminate spelling and grammatical errors. At this point there is a high degree of confidence that the copy is errorless and is ready to be converted to type. An input medium is prepared and the type is set. The output or galleys are proofread, comparing the output to the original. Errors are noted and corrections are made.

Error Detection and Elimination

The oldest method of detecting errors is by proofreading. A proofreader, knowledgeable in the rules of English grammar, spelling, and typographic style, carefully compares the typeset galley to the original manuscript. A special set of proofreader's symbols, shown in Figure 1, are used to indicate errors. Copy reading, a more effective form of proofreading is frequently used in the preparation of legal texts. Copy reading requires two proofreaders, one reading the manuscript aloud while the other follows on the typeset galley. While this method more efficiently eliminates errors it also doubles the proofreading costs.

Figure 1. *Proofreader's marks used to indicate errors in original copy or typeset galleys.*

Editing Devices

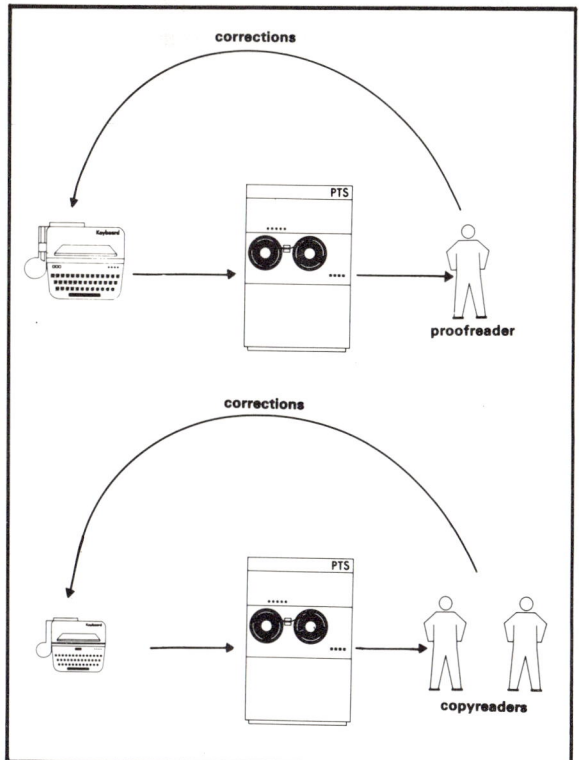

Author's Alterations

Another form of error detection is by the examination of the typeset galley by the author himself. The author may or may not be effective at locating errors, but whether he is or is not, he is seeing his manuscript set in type for the first time, and may decide to make major changes. Such changes made to galley proofs are called author's alterations ("aa"s) and are usually the most costly changes, because they are the most major.

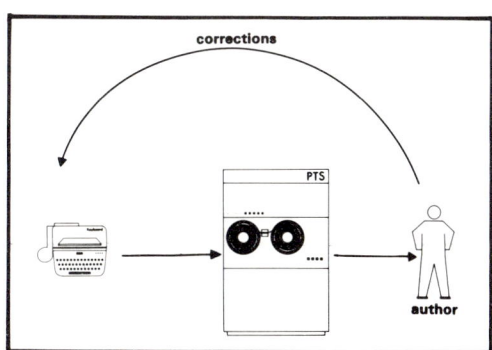

Corrections

Once errors have been found, regardless of the detection method used, a correction procedure must be used. The correction will be either to the existing galley, or to the input medium, to produce a new, error-free galley. Correcting the existing galley requires that the corrections be set and pasted-over or cut-into exact position. Correcting the input medium can be done by either the machine-merging of the existing recording medium and a correction medium, or by the manual-merging method of cutting and inserting called *splicing*.

Splicing tape

The best method of error detection is one which permits the location of errors *before* the type is set. Such a method saves time, labor, and materials. As early as 1887, Tolbert Lanston, the inventor of the Monotype, had proposed the direct keyboarding of manuscripts by authors themselves to eliminate the errors inherent in re-keyboarding. This idea was again proposed when TTS keyboards became widespread, but met with similar resistance.

Blind, non-counting Keyboards

Most perforating keyboards in use today are blind and non-counting. This has two effects on error rate. First, because the operator is not distracted by a visual display nor by end-of-line decisions, he can output more words per minute. Generally speaking, the higher the output speed, the greater the error rate. Second, because there is no visual display, it is easier for the operator to make an error should he lose his place, or run out of tape or be distracted or whatever.°

Use of a Computer

One method of finding errors in unjustified tape prior to typesetting is by use of a computer. Using a specially programmed computer, perforated or mag-

---

°*Visual keyboards, although a distraction, help the operator detect errors as they happen. Visuals include hard copy, floating display, last code or last character display, and dual image.*

Editing Devices

netic tape can be input, and numbered, justified lines can be output via a high speed line printer. The output is proofread, and a correction tape, keyed to the numbered lines containing errors, is prepared and merged with the original tape. The result is an errorless or clean tape ready for typesetting.

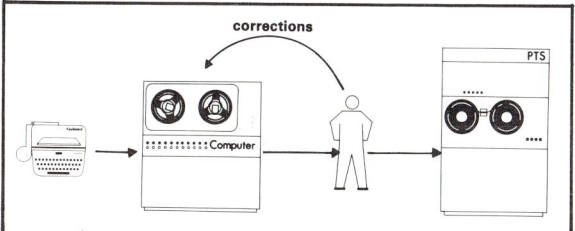

Another use of the computer is for a method called *double keyboarding*. It is based on the belief that two people do not make exactly the same mistakes. Two perforator operators key the same copy. Their tapes are compared by the computer, which stops and displays the words or sentences which disagree. A monitor or proofreader chooses the correct entry and the process continues. The result again is a clean tape.

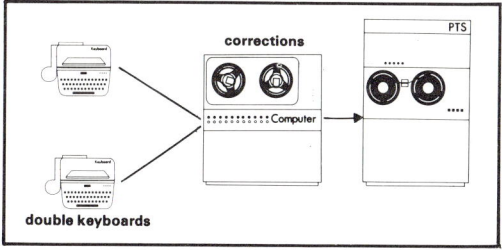

The VDT

An increasingly popular method of producing clean tapes is by use of a VDT: Visual Display Terminal. A VDT is, very simply, a TV for words rather than pictures. It is capable of interpreting and displaying magnetic or perforated codes as human-readable characters across the face of a cathode-ray tube (CRT). An integrated keyboard is used to enter alphanumeric characters, insert typographic functions, and enter editing commands. A keyboard layout of the Mergenthaler CorRecTerm editing terminal is shown in Figure 2.

A VDT can be used to electronically perform what is done by either an editor or a proofreader. For this reason a VDT is sometimes referred to as an electronic editing device, a text proofing device, a text editing device, a proofreader, or a videotypewriter. Regardless of its name, most VDTs perform the same functions, which include:

deleting (removing) characters, words, lines, or blocks of copy.

adding (inserting) characters, words, lines, or blocks of copy.

Understanding Phototypesetting

replacing (writing over) characters, words, lines or blocks of copy.

changing job parameters (line lengths, point sizes, type styles, line leading, etc.).

There are many different VDTs on the market, most of which are off-line (single-station application), stand-alone units. Major differences are related to the size of the computer memory and, therefore, the capacity of the visual display screen. The larger the computer memory, the greater the editing capabilities and storage. Also, in large printing plants and newspapers, several VDTs may be wired to a single large computer called a controller to form a high powered system.

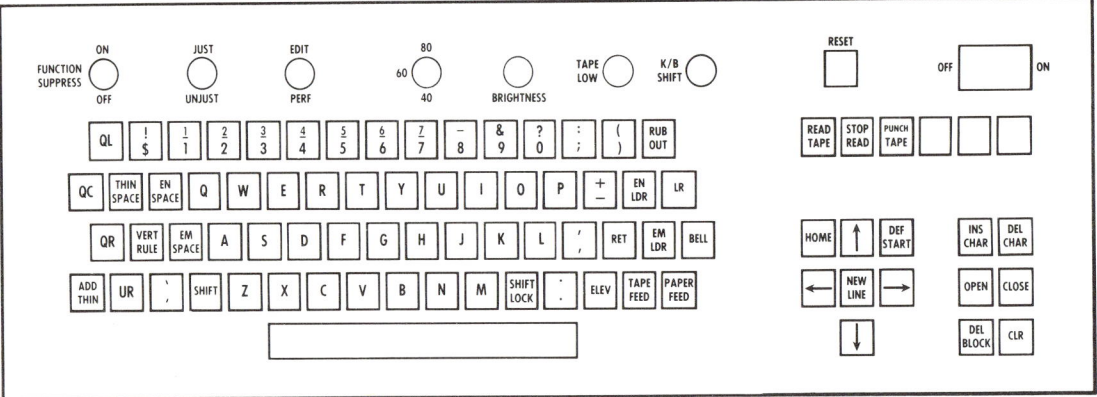

Figure 2. The keyboard layout of the Mergenthaler CorRecTerm editing terminal.

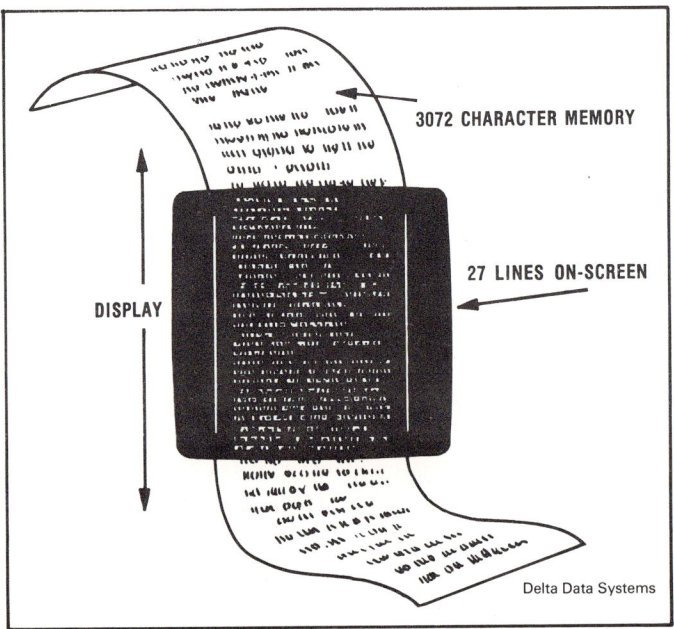

Figure 3. The scrolling technique holds lines in memory until the operator is ready to review and/or change them. Courtesy of Delta Data Systems Corporation.

Editing Devices

VDTs are usually evaluated on the basis of their screen and memory capacities. Some VDTs have no memory other than their screen display. Others have expandable memories large enough for the storage of thousands of characters. A machine which has a memory limited to the screen display would output (to tape) the top one or two lines each time the bottom line is completed.

A machine with a memory storage area is capable of storing lines that have already been edited, and of reviewing those lines. This ability to move, or roll lines up and down prior to outputting is called scrolling. The scrolling concept is illustrated in Figure 3.

Use of a VDT

In their initial use in the data processing field they were called "data windows," and today, in their modified graphic arts form, visual display terminals are considered windows on the phototypesetting system. This window on the system is capable of performing three major functions. First, tapes can be proofed and edited prior to typesetting. Corrections can be made and machine parametes can be changed. Second, previously run tapes can be updated, new material inserted, and obsolete material deleted. Third, the VDT can be used as a source of original input. In this mode the machine is used as a videotypewriter.

In its most popular configuration the VDT is the middleman between the blind keyboard and the phototypesetter.

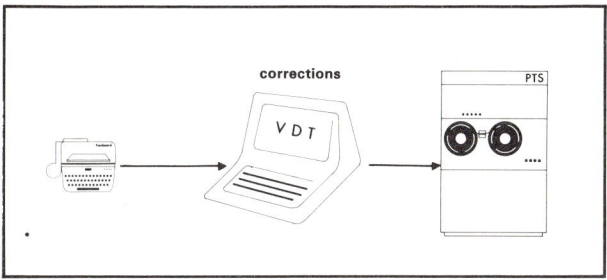

Tape produced on the blind keyboard is read on the VDT tape reader and displayed character-by-character or line-by-line on the face of the CRT. The characters are monospaced, each character, regardless of its relative width, occupying the same rectangular space. The operator can add, delete, or replace any character on the screen by positioning a flickering rectangle of light or a character underline called the cursor. The cursor is a placemarker which the operator can move in practically any direction to alter the character display on the screen. The cursor controls for the Singer 9400 are shown in Figure 4. A demonstration of the use of the cursor on the screen of the Vari-Typer Electro/Set 450 is shown in Figure 5.

Understanding Phototypesetting

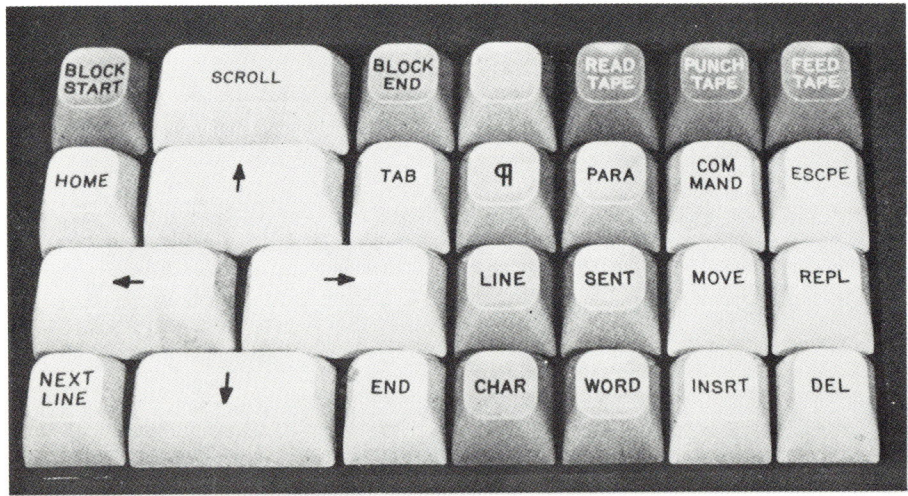

Figure 4. The cursor control keys on the Singer 9400 editing terminal.

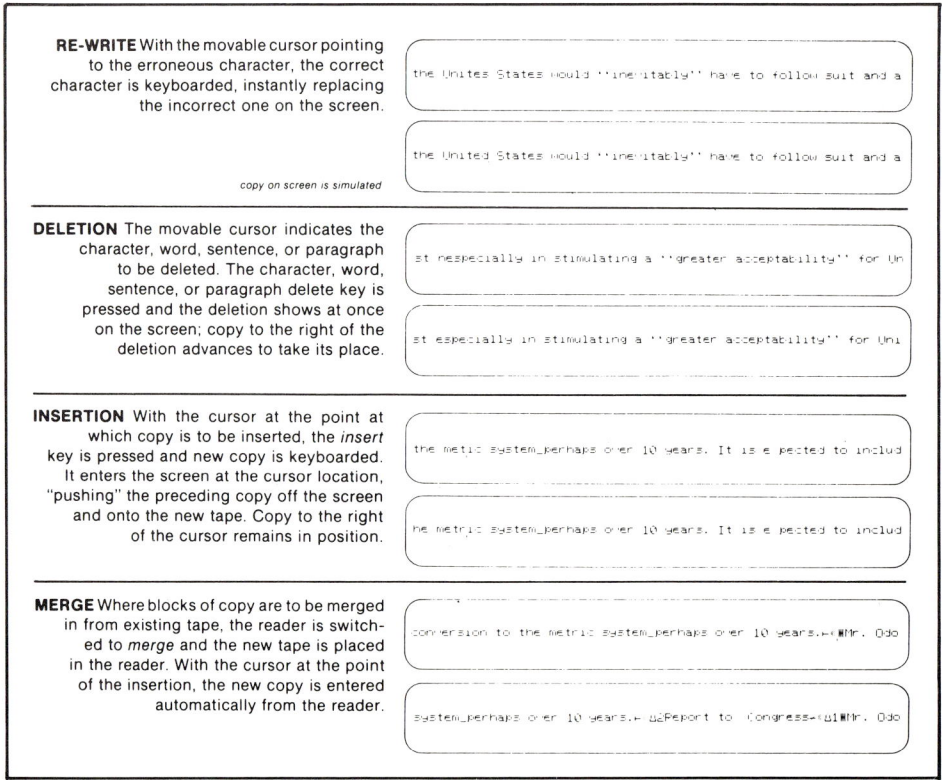

Figure 5. The cursor controls the point of editing activity as shown on the VariTyper Electro/Set 450.

HOME	Drives cursor to Home position (top left corner of screen).
(Cursor Up) Key	Drives cursor up one line for each pressure. Inhibited if cursor is already in top line (top line of column 1 in double-column format).
DEF START Key	When pressed, current cursor position is defined as start of punch or delete block operation. Cursor must then be moved to indicate end of operation.
(Cursor Left) Key	Drives cursor one character position left for each pressure. Inhibited if cursor is already in leftmost position of line or column.
NEW LINE Key	Drives cursor to start of next line.
(Cursor Right) Key	Drives cursor one character position right for each pressure. Inhibited when cursor reaches end of screen.
(Cursor Down) Key	Drives cursor down one line for each pressure. Inhibited when cursor reaches bottom line (bottom line of column 2 in double-column format).
INS CHAR Key	The character at the cursor position and all characters to the right of it are moved one position right; a null is inserted at the cursor position. The function is inhibited if the shift would move any character except a space into the last position of the line.
DEL CHAR Key	The character at the cursor position is deleted and all characters to the right of the cursor are moved one position left. A null is inserted in the last position of the line.
OPEN Key	All characters from the cursor position to the end of text are recopied starting at the end of screen and building up. In double-column format, the material is moved to the end of column 2.
CLOSE Key	Material at the bottom of the screen is recopied, starting at the cursor position. This closes any gap left after insertion of new material; the wraparound feature prevents the breaking of words at line endings.
DEL BLOCK Key	Erases all characters between a previously defined Start (or the Home position if no Start was defined) and the current cursor position. The gap is closed.
CLR Key	Erases all characters from the current cursor position to end of screen. Nulls are inserted in the erased positions.

Table 1. The cursor and editing controls for the Mergenthaler CorRecTerm Visual Display Terminal.

Understanding Phototypesetting

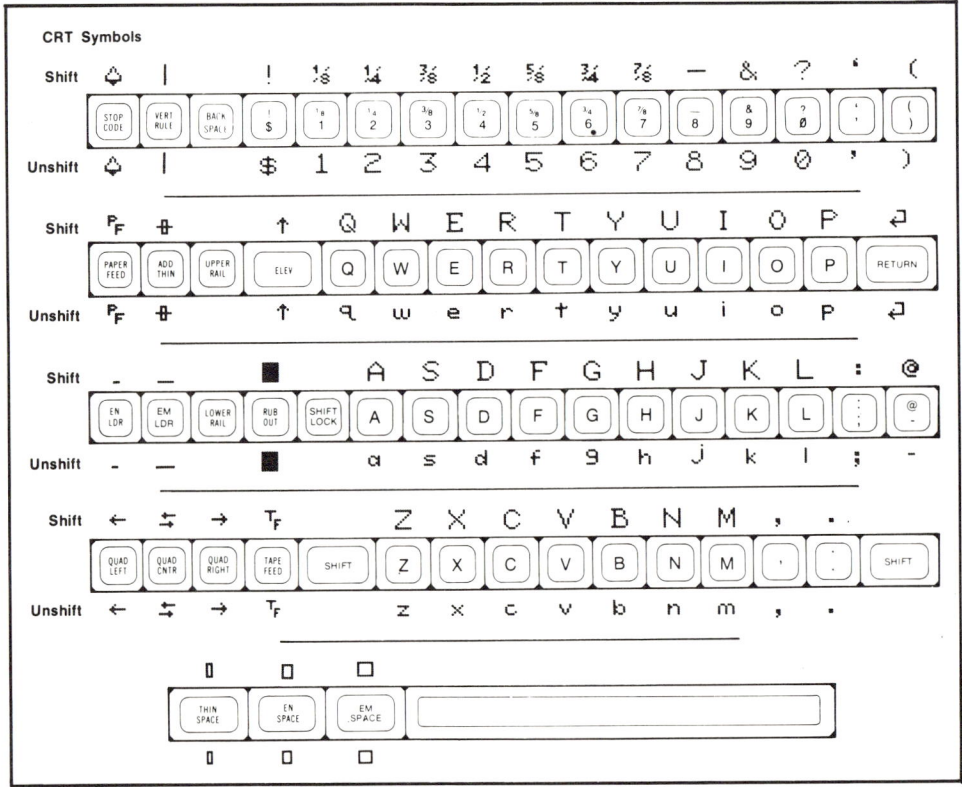

Figure 6. The Singer 9400 VDT keyboard layout with the corresponding CRT symbols.

The size of the characters on the screen is constant, regardless of the size which the characters will take when they are typeset.° The type size varies from one machine to another, from 12 points (Mohrtext) up to 20 points (Hendrix). Figure 6 shows the keyboard layout of the Singer 9400 VDT with the CRT symbols as they are actually displayed on the screen.

The actual operation of a VDT varies somewhat from machine to machine, yet the major functions are fairly constant and similar. The cursor and editing controls for the CorRecTerm VDT are shown in Table 1.

Evaluation of a visual display terminal requires some consideration of the following features:

Screen capacity - total number of characters which can be displayed on the screen (number of characters per line ×number of lines)

Storage (memory) capacity - number of characters which can be held in memory prior to, or following their display on the CRT.

°*The exception is the Harris 2200 which displays point sizes from 6 to 48 points on the VDT screen. See the section titled "CAM."*

Format - single and/or double column mode(s).

Wraparound - ability of a VDT to take words or parts of words which exceed one line and carry them over to the next.
Character set - the total number of screen-displayable symbols.
Character size - the point size of the CRT font, usually between 12 and 20 points.
Viewing area - the size of the CRT screen.
Cursor - blinking light or character underline. Single step, continuous, up, down, right, left, diagonal, home, next line.
Editing functions - overstrike, insert (add), delete for character, line or block.
Text scroll - single line and continuous.
Input device options - paper tape reader, magnetic tape reader, OCR, direct keyboard.
Output device options - paper tape, magnetic tape, on-line to phototypesetter.

CAM

A VDT which is capable of displaying characters in the point size and character width in which they will be set is called a Composition and Make-up Terminal (CAM). One commercially available system is the Harris 2200 Video Layout Terminal as shown in Figure 7.

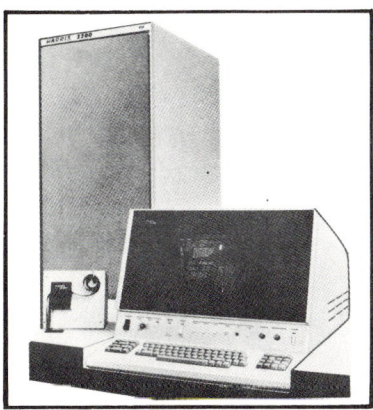

Figure 7. The Harris 2200 is a composition and make-up terminal displaying copy on its CRT exactly as it will appear when typeset.

Matrix Proofers

Versatec Corporation manufactures two high speed (300-500 lines per minute) line printers for proofing either on-line with a computer or off-line with paper tape. The machines operate on an electrostatic writing principle called MEWT, for Matrix Electrostatic Writing Technique. Characters are formed by the application of a liquid toner to a minute series of electrostatic dots which are placed on the paper by selective charges from a writing head. Figure 8 shows the path which the paper travels during the image creation. Figure 9 shows a single matrix character as formed by the precision application of toner, as well as a sample of lines as they would appear for proofreading.

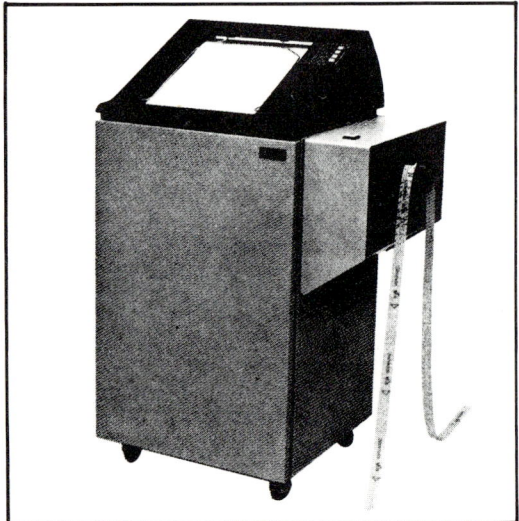

Matrix 1616PTR Proofer

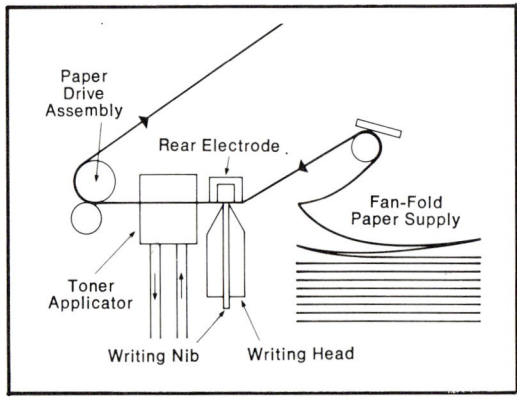

Figure 8. The operating principle of a matrix proofer.

Editing Devices

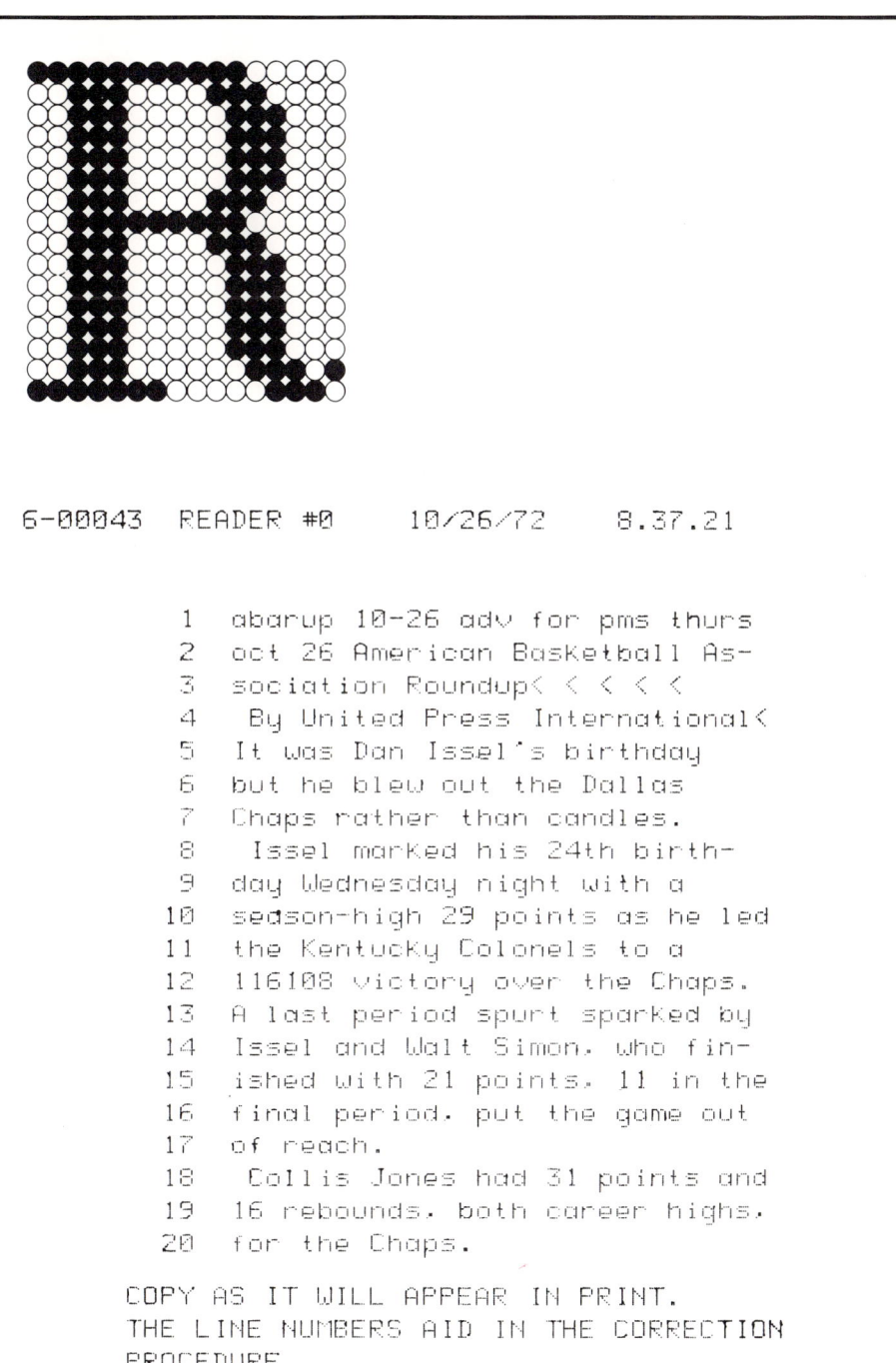

Figure 9. A 16x16 dot matrix is used on the Veratec 1616P. The faster model 1150P uses a 7x9 dot matrix. Actual lines appear below. Line numbers aid in the correction procedure.

VDT Manufacturers

Specific information related to VDT models may be had by writing directly to the manufacturer. The names and addresses of the major equipment suppliers follow:

Addressograph-Multigraph Corporation
Varityper Division
11 Mount Pleasant Avenue
East Hanover, New Jersey 07936

Automix Keyboards Inc. (AKI)
4200 150th N.E.
Redmond, Washington 98052

CompuScan Inc.
900 Huyler Street
Teterboro, New Jersey 07608

Delta-Data Systems Corporation
Woodhaven Industrial Park
Cornwells Heights, Pennsylvania 19020

Graphic Systems Inc.
217 Jackson Street
Lowell, Massachusetts 01852

Harris Corporation
P.O. Box 2080
Melbourne, Florida 32901

Hendrix Electronics Incorporated
695 Harvey Road
Manchester, New Hampshire 03103

ICS Sales and Leasing Incorporated
P.O. Box 281
313 North 1st Street
Ann Arbor, Michigan 48107

Imlac Corporation
150 A Street
New England Industrial Center
Needham, Massachusetts 02194

Lexicon Incorporated
60 Turner Street
Waltham, Massachusetts 02154

Mergenthaler Linotype Company
One Mergenthaler Drive
Plainview, New York 11803

Editing Devices

Newcaxton
Lincoln Highway East 5
Gettysburg, Pennsylvania 17325

Newspaper Electronics Corporation
7948 Wornall
Kansas City, Missouri 64114

Star Graphic Systems Incorporated
240 South Main Street
South Hackensack, New Jersey 07606

The Singer Company
Singer Graphic Systems Division
151 Callan Ave
San Leandro, California 94577

Varisystems Corporation
207 Newton Road
Plainview, New York 11803

Video Graphics Incorporated
One Town Hall Square
Nutley, New Jersey 07110

6 phototypesetting machines

Summary

Phototypesetting refers to a high speed method of setting automatically justified lines of text using photographic principles. There are currently three generations of machines, so named to distinguish between three stages of development. The *first generation* machines are modified hot metal typesetters which substitute a camera for the casting mechanism. The *second generation* machines are characterized by electromechanical devices which increase their efficiency and speed, and reduce their cost. The *third generation* machines utilize cathode-ray tube (CRT) technology to set entire pages of type in a matter of minutes.

Most phototypesetters in use today are second generation machines. The basic components of their operation include a high intensity light source, a negative film image carrier, a lens system, and a length of photographic material. The font may take the form of a *disc, drum, film strip, turret,* or *grid*.

Third generation phototypesetters flash characters on the face of a CRT and expose them through a lens onto photographic material. Fonts are stored either on a negative grid, or digitally on magnetic tape.

Phototypesetting machine capabilities vary, and are evaluated on the basis of maximum line length, number of typefaces, number of point sizes, maximum leading, method of hyphenation and justification, and speed.

The general trend toward phototypesetting can be attributed to a number of advantages over other typesetting systems. Among these advantages are lower initial cost, higher speed, greater size range, more input options, less floor space, less skilled operators, elimination of galley storage, greater character repertoire, less noise, and less machine heat.

Trade Terms

character repertoire - the total number of displayable characters in each font, in each style, in each point size.

character set - the alphanumeric symbols, punctuation, and special characters of a single font.

CRT (Cathrode-Ray Tube) - an electronic device resembling a television tube which is used in high-speed photocomposition to flash character images onto film, paper, microfilm or offset plates. The CRT image is composed of extremely fine dots or lines.

dictionary look-up - a method of machine hyphenation utilizing a computer stored dictionary.

digital storage - a method of storing font information for the generation of CRT characters.

disc - a round glass plate used in some second generation phototypesetters as an image master.

drum - a circular metal plate around which are wrapped film strip image masters. This method of font storage is unique to second generation phototypesetters.

exception dictionary - a computer stored list of user chosen words which are frequently hyphenated incorrectly by the phototypesetter logic program.

film advance - downward movement of the photographic material so as to allow for the composition of the next line.

film strip - a flexible phototypesetter image master with transparent typographic characters appearing on an opaque black background.

first generation - those phototypesetting machines which were based on photomechanical principles incorporated in modified linecaster design.

galley - a section of photographic material carrying typeset matter for proofing or make-up.

grid - a stationary, evenly illuminated character master used in second and third generation phototypesetters.

image master - the photographic negative form in which a phototypesetter font is carried. These forms include disc, drum, turret, and matrix.

increment - a fixed repeatable measurement. Film advance or leading is specified as a multiple factor of the minimum leading increment.

laser (light amplification by stimulated emission of radiation) - an intense beam of light used experimentally for high speed phototypesetting.

lens turret - a metal disc housing lenses of various magnifying powers used to generate point size changes in some first and second generation phototypesetters.

media carriage - that part of a phototypesetter which houses the photographic material.

photocomposition - a method of setting completely made-up ads or pages.

photolettering - the production of display material or custom typography by manual or semi-automated means.

phototypesetting - the rapid composition of typographic characters onto photographic film or paper for graphic reproduction. Characters are projected through negative image masters or generated on the face of a high resolution CRT.

reverse leading - the opposite of film advance. Permits the backward movement of the photographic material. See film advance.

second generation - those phototypesetting machines using electromechanical principles.

size range - the span of point sizes from smallest to largest which a phototypesetter is capable of setting.

third generation - those phototypesetters using CRT principles.

tick mark - an optical timing mark used to indicate the locations of characters on certain image masters.

turret - an hourglass shaped image master.

zoom lens - a lens assembly capable of producing a wide range of magnification powers (i.e. point sizes).

Introduction

Machines which set type photographically fall into three rather indistinct categories: photolettering, phototypesetting and photocomposing. Photolettering machines are generally slow, manual devices used to produce custom display typography. Phototypesetting machines are high speed devices usually producing straight text. Photocomposing machines are those which are capable of high speed composition of whole pages or areas of composition. While some typesetting machines neatly fit into one of these classifications, many do not. For this reason, machines in this unit will be collectively termed "phototypesetting" devices.

The Basic Components

A phototypesetter is basically a camera which is capable of projecting alphanumeric symbols onto a photographic material at great speed. The earliest methods, termed first generation, were modifications of existing hot metal typesetters. The introduction of electromechanical devices characterized the second generation of phototypesetters, and the cathode-ray tube (CRT) characterized the third. The vast majority of phototypesetters in use today operate on second generation principles.

The first component of a second generation phototypesetter is a high intensity light source (usually xenon):

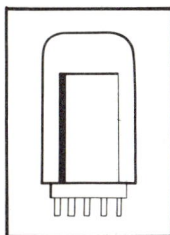

which is located behind a negative film image;

which is located behind a lens;

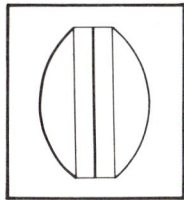

which is focused on the surface of photographic material.

As the required characters are brought into position before the light source they are flashed through the lens and onto the photographic material. The spacing of characters along a line is accomplished by either:
1. moving the lens, or
2. rotating a mirror which is used to deflect the image, or
3. moving the light source and master, or
4. moving the media carriage (paper or film).

In the first instance, the lens moves, scanning the stationary photographic material character by character to compose lines.

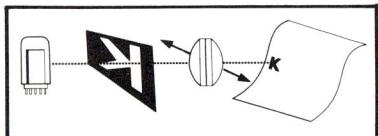

In the second case, a rotating mirror or prism deflects the image across the width of the photographic paper or film.

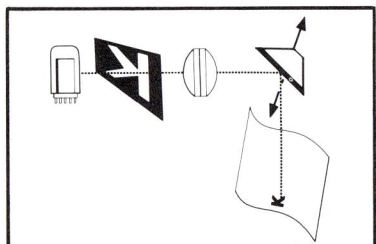

A third possibility is moving both the light source and the image master to set characters across a page.

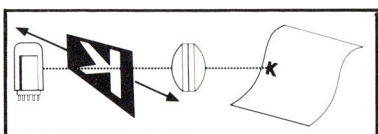

Another method of positioning characters horizontally is by moving the media carriage which holds the photographic material.

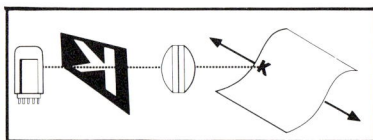

Vertical positioning of characters is similar in all second generation systems, namely, by advancing the photographic material. This movement is sometimes called film advance, line spacing, line advance, or leading. Some machines have a provision for moving the photo material backward called reverse leading.

Image Masters

The character sets, fonts, or masters used in second generation machines are film negatives, that is, transparent images with opaque backgrounds. These character sets take four basic configurations:

1. Disc. Typefaces may be arranged in concentric circles around the circumference of a glass disc. This disc turns at great speed, flashing one character with each rotation. Discs for any one machine are interchangeable (see Figure 1).

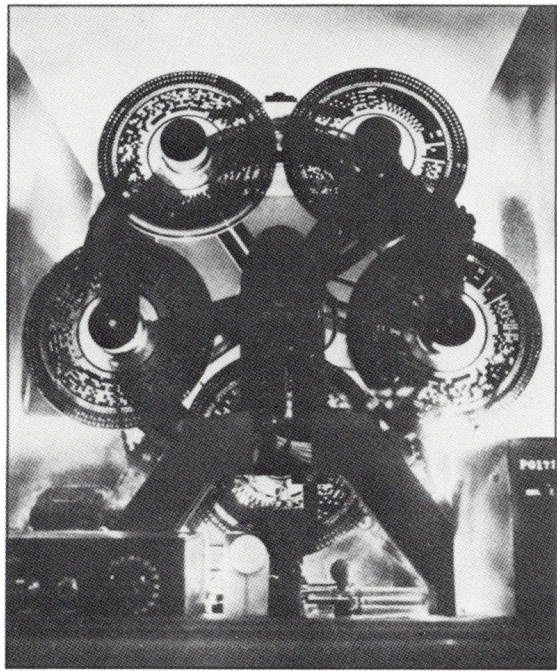

Figure 1. The Harris Fototronic uses a five-disc array.

The exact flashing of each character is accomplished by the use of transparent timing marks or tick marks aligned with each character. The computer logic of the machine is not capable of identifying the characters themselves, but it is capable of identifying their serial locations. When an *e* code, for example, is entered into the machine it is interpreted as being in, say, the fifth position. A photoelectric cell senses or counts five tick marks and then triggers the light source to flash the character which is directly before it, in this case the *e*.

2. Drum. One or more font strips may be wrapped around a circular metal drum or font wheel. A light source is positioned within the spinning drum and flashes characters by the same method as the disc. (See Figure 2.)

Understanding Phototypesetting

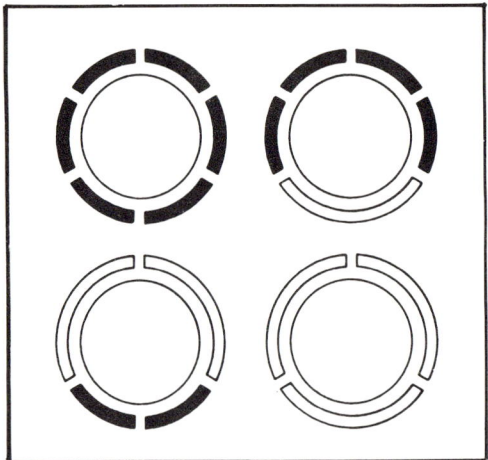
Four ways of "dressing" the Mergenthaler V.I.P. font drum.

Figure 2. The font wheel on the CompuWriter Jr.

If there are two font strips, one is usually designated as the upper magazine (UM) and the other as the lower magazine (LM). This terminology is derived from the use of multiple font magazines on a linecasting machine.

Phototypesetting Machines

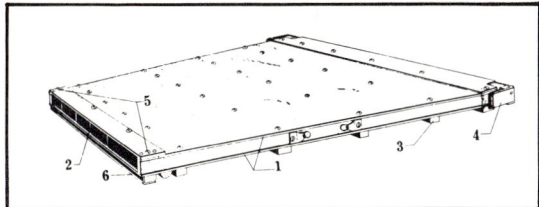
An Intertype magazine.

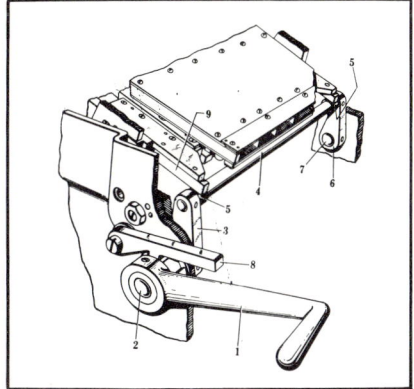
Upper and lower magazines on an Intertype Mixer linecaster.

If there is more than one font on a single film strip, they may be differentiated as being in lower and upper rail (LR, UR) positions, again terms derived from linecasting operation.

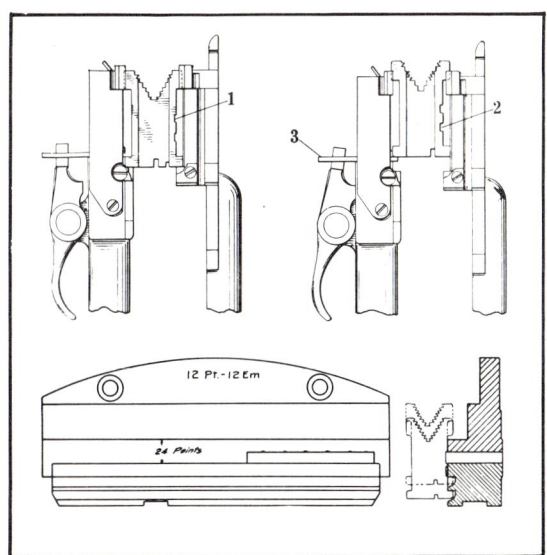
Lower and upper rail positions on the Intertype linecaster.

107

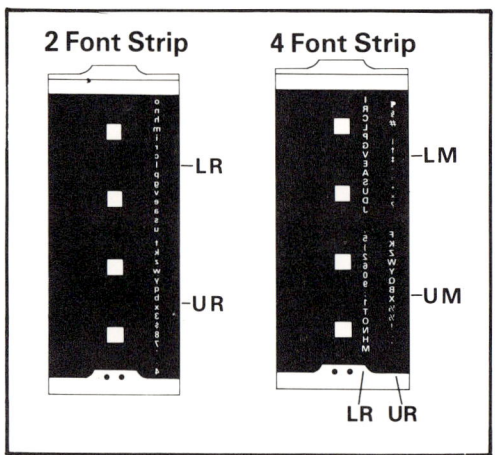

3. Grid. Grids are stationary, evenly illuminated character masters. Light rays traveling through each character are made parallel by a series of lenses called a collimator assembly. The rays then enter a series of optical wedges which form a configuration to isolate a single character.

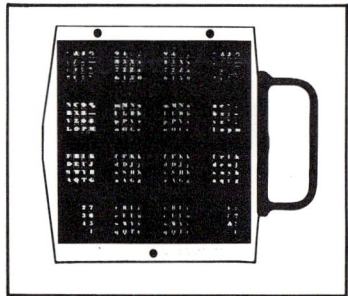

4. Turret. A no-longer-used image master is the hourglass shaped turret. The light source was located inside the spinning cylinder.

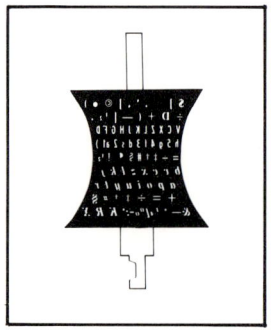

Point Size

The actual size of image characters on font masters, whether disc, drum, turret, or grid is about 5 points. Increasing, and occasionally decreasing, that size is accomplished by one of four basic methods:

1. Manual. The lens used to focus the image on the photographic material is manually changed for one of greater or lesser power.

2. Turret. Lenses of varying magnification are arranged in circular fashion around a precision metal disc. Each lens represents a different point size and can be automatically changed by a key stroke (direct entry) or a tape code.

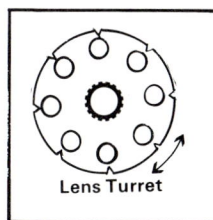

3. Zoom. A lens assembly capable of multiple magnifications is called a zoom lens. Such a system operates automatically by keyboard or tape signals. (See Figure 3.)

4. Font. The font master itself may be replaced with one with larger size original images.

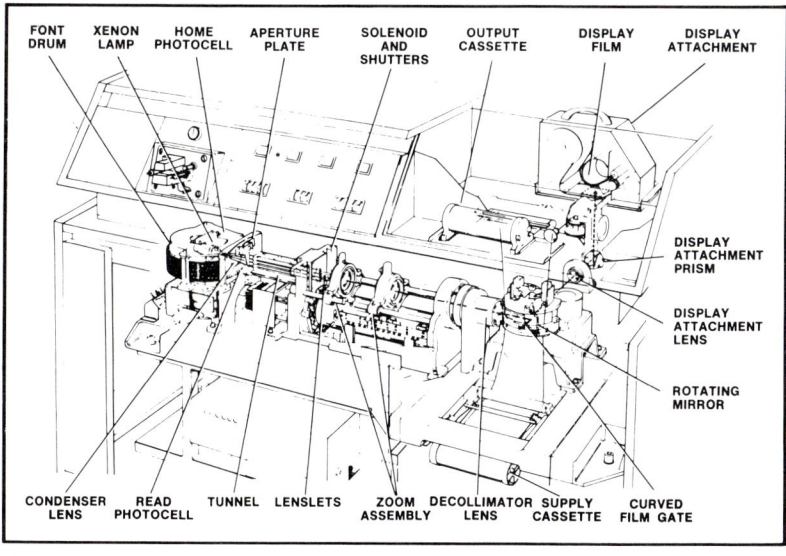

Figure 3. Schematic drawing of the Mergenthaler V-I-P optical system. Type sizes are changed by movement of the zoom lens assembly.

The First Generation

Offset lithography, sometimes called "photo offset," is a method of printing which uses a light-formed image on a film negative to produce a light-formed image on a printing plate. The use of lithography increased following World War II, and with it the interest in a compatible photographic typesetting system. The typesetting workhorses of that time were the Linotype and the Monotype. To use type set on these machines for offset reproduction meant "pulling proofs"—making single-impression press copies suitable for photographing. A machine capable of producing a photographic output would eliminate the proofing stage.

A linecasting machine very similar to the Linotype is the Intertype. In 1947, the Intertype Corporation (now the Harris Corporation) introduced the *Fotosetter*, a modified linecaster which used circulating negative image masters (matrices), and substituted a camera (Figure 4) for the hot-metal casting mechanism (Figure 5). This machine is considered the first phototypesetter. Soon afterward the Monotype machine was modified with a negative image grid and a camera and renamed the Monophoto (Figure 6).

The first generation machines are characterized as fairly slow, mechanical devices having many of the same operating principles of their parent machines. It is estimated that over 700 Fotosetters have been sold at a cost of $33,000 each, and 300 Monophotos at an individual cost of $20,750.

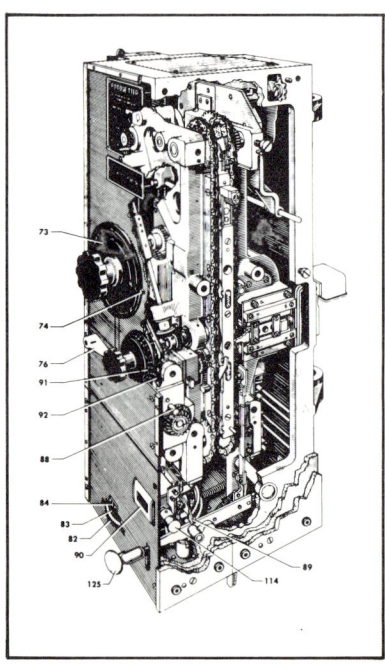

Figure 4. The Fotosetter camera which replaced the hot metal casting mechanism. (Numbers are keyed to the training manual text.)

Phototypesetting Machines

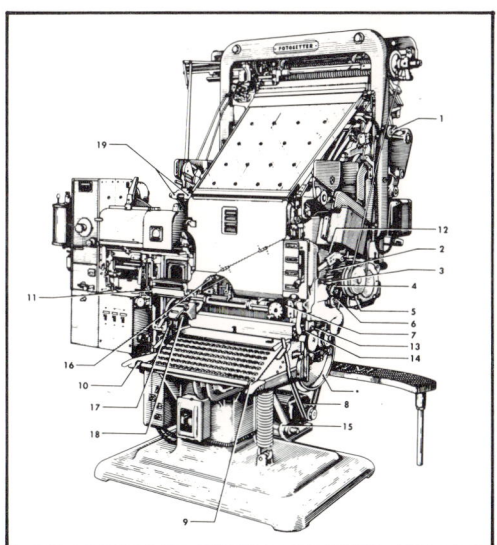

Figure 5. The Intertype Fotosetter resembles a linecasting machine. The camera is shown on the extreme left. Also see Figure 4. (Numbers refer to lubrication points.)

Figure 6. The Monophoto phototypesetter replaced the hot metal casting mechanism with a camera assembly.

The Development of the Second Generation Machine

The first true second-generation machine, the Photon 200, made its appearance in 1956. Some ten years before, two French inventors, R. Higonnet and L. Moyroud, had begun its development, and secured financing from American sources. The machine typified the second-generation characteristics of speed and electromechanical operation. A brief chronological listing of second-generation machines follows:

1956—*Photon 200*, rotating glass disc, lens turret, typewriter hard copy, $50,000, about 300 sold.

1958—American Type Founders (ATF) - *ATF Typesetter*, keyboard perforator and photo unit, 7 models, 900 photo units and 1100 keyboards sold for between $10,000 to $20,000 each.

1958—Mergenthaler - *Linofilm*, keyboard and photo unit, 300 photo units and 600 keyboards sold, about $57,000 for one of each.

1959—Filmotype - *Alphatype*, magnetic tape input, photo unit and keyboard, 800 sold, $16,500 complete.

1961—Photon - *Model 713*, font drum, compatible with all tape perforating keyboards and computers, 500 sold, $40,000 each.

1964—Intertype - *Fototronic*, $54,000 photo unit, $19,000 keyboard.

1964—Mergenthaler - *Linofilm Quick*, font grid, 350 sold at approximately $30,000 each.

1966—Photon - *Zip* - font grid and flash tubes, $250,000 each.

1967—Fairchild - *PhotoTextSetter 2000*, turret font, 150 sold, $17,950 each.

1968—Mergenthaler - *Linofilm Super Quick*, $30,000.

1968—Intertype - *Fototronic 1200*, five discs, $62,500.

The Third Generation

The development of high speed phototypesetters using cathode-ray tube technology was a result of a need for a quality alternative to computer print-out composition. The first CRT typesetter, the *Digiset*, was introduced in West Germany in 1966. It was capable of generating up to 1200 characters per second on the face of its CRT. Marketing rights had been purchased by RCA in 1964, and the system was sold in the United States as the *Videocomp*. RCA phased out its Graphic Systems division in 1971 when it proved unprofitable. An example of Digiset characters is shown in Figure 7.

Phototypesetting Machines

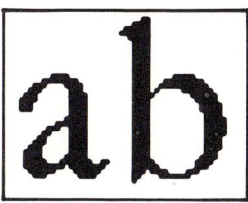

Figure 7. Digiset characters greatly enlarged.

    Commercial television in the United States uses a CRT with 525 horizontal lines on its screen, regardless of its diagonal picture size. CRT typesetters, however, use a highly refined tube with as many as 1800 vertical or horizontal strokes (lines) to the inch. Characters may be generated on the CRT surface in one of two ways. First, as in second-generation phototypesetting, the character may be in grid form (Figure 8). In this system two CRTs are used, one to scan the character grid and transmit its "picture," the second to display the character before the photographic material. The second method is by storing the characters digitally on magnetic tape. In this system, coded information is used to describe character shape in terms of the position and length of minute strokes of electrons. The letter *H*, for example could be coded as follows,

Start	Stop
A1	A2
A10	A11
B1	B11
C1	C2
C6	C7
C10	C11
D6	D7
E6	E7
F1	F2
F6	F7
F10	F11
G1	G11
H1	H2
H10	H11

and displayed like this:

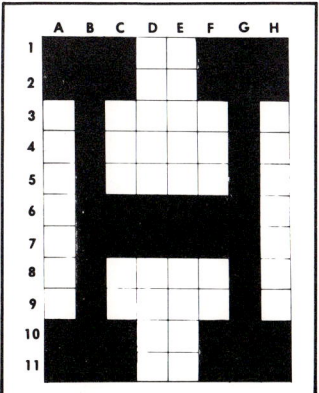

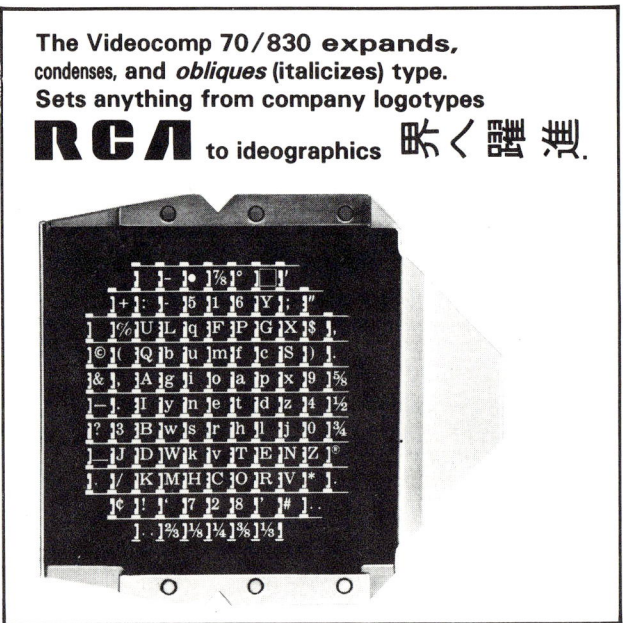

Figure 8. A Compugraphic VideoSetter image master grid.

Input to CRT phototypesetters is usually by magnetic tape because of its high input speed, although perforated tape is also used. Systems using digitized character generation often require additional storage area usually in the form of peripheral magnetic discs.

CRT typesetters are capable of electronically modifying characters within the limits of their assigned set-widths. Characters can be automatically expanded, condensed and sloped (italicized), with no reduction in through-put speed. Point-size changes are accomplished by electronic magnification.

Major manufacturers of CRT phototypesetters include Hell (Digiset), Mergenthaler (Linotron 1010, 505, 303), Harris (Fototronic CRT), and Compugraphic (Videosetter). Today the CRT represents the most expensive yet most productive means of quality typesetting. It is estimated that a CRT phototypesetter is capable of out-producing over 100 linecasters. Yet, even as some CRT typesetters are crunching out an excess of 10,000 characters per second, research is being conducted into laser (*l*ight *a*mplification by *s*timulated *e*mission of *r*adiation) technology to produce still faster and more efficient machines.

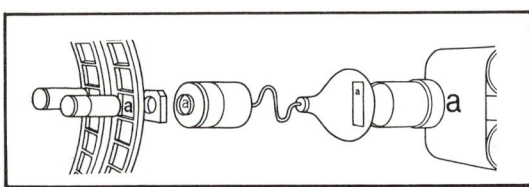

A diagram of the Crossfield Cathode-Ray Tube image generator.

Machine Capabilities

Just as linecasting machines were developed to automate the composition of type for the relief printing process, so have phototypesetting machines been designed to produce type for the offset lithographic process. The capabilities of a phototypesetter can be expressed in the same terms used to describe the functions of a linecaster.

The line length or measure is expressed in picas, and typically ranges from a low limit of 33 picas to a high of 100 picas, with the average maximum line length equal to about 45 picas. The output medium, either film or paper is available in a variety of widths, from 3 inches through 17 inches, with different specifications required for almost every machine.

Typefaces vary in number, size, and design. Some phototypesetters are limited to a single typeface, while CRT models using digital storage are capable of accessing over 200 typefaces at any time. The average second generation machine has between four and eight typefaces all of which can be mixed at any point in a line. The number of characters in each font also varies from one machine to another, from a low of 82 to a high of over 200. Most fonts have between 100 and 130 characters. Some machines have a provision for *pi characters*, which are special characters or symbols not usually found in the standard font.

The variety of typeface designs also varies from one manufacturer to the next. Mergenthaler and Intertype, two companies with a large investment in hot metal type design have each converted over 1000 typefaces to photographic image form. Photon, the oldest phototypesetter manufacturer has a library of about 600 typefaces. All other manufacturers have far fewer, some less than a handful.

Popular type designs have been imitated by almost every phototypesetting machine manufacturer. The result is that the Photon Bodoni may be different from the Alphatype Bodoni. Another problem is that many manufacturers, in an attempt to market their interpretation of a popular typeface, change its name. Melior, a Hermann Zapf design, is sold as Uranus by Alphatype, Mallard by Compugraphic, Ventura by Graphic Systems and Singer, Medallion by Intertype, Ballardvale by Photon, Lyra by Star, and Hanover by VariTyper.

The span of type sizes which a machine is capable of setting, from its smallest size to its largest, is called the *point-size range*. This range may spread from as small as 4 points to as large as 144 points, with as many as twenty different sizes in between. A few CRT machines are capable of setting as many as 680 different point sizes due to the flexibility of electronic magnification. Most second generation phototypesetters, however, have between four and sixteen point sizes available, with the average being about twelve.

Leading or film advance is also specified in terms of a range. The maximum film advance varies from one machine to the next, from 14-3/4 points to 499 points and more. The exact amount of leading or line spacing required for each line is determined as a multiple of a fixed increment or step. The most common increment is 1/2-point, and in this case, leading can be noted as X number of 1/2-point increments, Other increments include 1-point, 1/4-point, 1/10-point, and 1/32-point.

H and J

Early phototypesetting machines required perforated tapes with all end-of-line information included (justified tape). These tapes could be prepared on a counting keyboard or by processing an unjustified tape through a computer. Today, the general trend is toward the placement of a computer inside the phototypesetter itself, with the machine calculating all line (justification) and word breaks (hyphenation). Justification is determined by adding character widths until the total approaches the justification zone. A 24-pica measure, for example, may accommodate 20-picas of character width. If there are eight spaces in the line, the space remaining at the end of the line would be evenly divided among those spaces.

$$\begin{aligned}\text{Measure} &= 24 \text{ pi} \\ \text{Total char. width} &= \underline{20 \text{ pi}} \\ \text{Excess space} &= 4 \text{ pi}\end{aligned}$$

Number of spaces = 8 pi

Additional interword space =
4 pi/8 spaces = 1/2 pica
(6 points) to be added
between each word
to justify the line

Justification is a fairly simple arithmetic process until it becomes necessary to break a word. Hyphenation becomes necessary when a word falling at the end of a line causes the line to exceed the justification range. In some cases the entire word can be carried to the next line, and its absence made up by word and letter spacing (hyphenless justification). This, however, gives the appearance of a very loose line, a poor typographic style. The alternative is to hyphenate the word and carry only part of it to the next line. Most phototypesetting machines accomplish this in one or more of three ways. First, when unjustified tape is prepared, the keyboard operator may anticipate some words which the computer can not differentiate, such as pre-sent, and pres-ent. The keyboard operator would insert a discretionary hyphen code at the proper point to make the break clear to the computer, should that particular word exceed the justification zone.

The second and most popular method of hyphenation is by the rules of English logic. The phototypesetter computer is programmed with information based upon grammatical usage. Such instructions include not breaking a word a) after less than two letters, b) so that three or less letters are carried to the next line, c) after a consonant followed by a vowel, d) before a punctuation mark, and many, many more. Logic programs are generally 98% accurate.

The third and most precise method of hyphenation is by dictionary look-up. An entire dictionary is stored on magnetic disc and consulted when necessary. Although this method is very effective, it is also very expensive, and requires continuous updating for new words. A variation of this method is an exception dictionary, a special collection of words which a particular company frequently encounters. The exception dictionary is used in conjunction with a logic program.

Speed

Phototypesetting machines are frequently evaluated on the basis of their ability to produce galleys of type. The word galley is borrowed from metal typesetting terminology where it means a flat metal tray used to store composed type. In a phototypesetting context, a galley is considered to be a section of processed output. The speed with which galleys are composed is usually stated in terms of characters per second (cps) or lines per minute (lpm). Characters per second is a deceptive measurement since it is dependent upon the size of the type being set: the larger the type, the fewer characters per second. Lines per minute is usually considered to be standard newspaper format, 8 to 9 point type on a 10- to 11-pica measure. Only when the point size and measure are known can the speed of one machine be compared to another. Also, frequent changes in point size and typeface substantially contribute to decreasing the speed of the machine.

Newspaper lines per minute range from 6 to well over 100, with CRT machines setting up to 4000 and more. The high speed of most CRT machines has brought the introduction of a new speed descriptor: pages per minute.

Knowing the number of characters per second, the characters per minute may be determined by multiplying by 60.

Characters per minute =
characters per second × 60

Since the average word measures five letters plus a space (in phototypesetting a space is a nonexposed escapement), the words per minute may be found by dividing the characters per minute by 6.

Words per minute =
characters per minute ÷ 6

The characters per hour is simply 60 times the characters per minute.

Characters per hour =
characters per minute × 60

Assuming an 8-point type size on an 11-pica measure with approximately 30 characters per line, the lines per minute may be determined by dividing the characters per minute by 30.

Lines per minute =
characters per minute ÷ 30

Finally, lines per hour may be found by multiplying lines per minute by 60.

Lines per hour =
lines per minute × 60

Advantages and Disadvantages of Phototypesetting

Today, most type is set by either photographic or hot metal methods. The general trend toward phototypesetting is a result of its numerous advantages over standard linecasting techniques. Among the advantages are:

Cost. A linecasting machine with less capability than most phototypesetters originally sold for over $35,000. In 1973, the average price of a phototypesetter was about $20,000, and the trend is toward lower priced yet equally or more flexible machines.

Speed. A tape-operated linecaster is capable of speeds ranging from 375 to 840 lines per hour, while a phototypesetter sets between 720 and 2400 and more lines per hour.

Size range. A linecaster requires a different magazine of matrices, or a different matrix case for each change in point size. A phototypesetter uses optics to change size from a single-image master.

Input options. Most linecasters which operate off-line use perforated tape. Phototypesetters utilize a variety of inputs including perforated tape, punched cards, 1/4" magnetic tape and magnetic cassettes.

Less floor space. Generally speaking, phototypesetting machines are more compact than their hot metal counterparts.

Less skilled operators. Both Linotype and Monotype machines utilize special keyboard layouts which require considerable practice and training. Most tape perforators on the other hand can be operated by trained office typists.

Elimination of galley storage. Jobs run on linecasting equipment, which are subject to reprinting, are often kept standing in galleys. Similar work produced by phototypesetting machines is kept either as pasted-up copy or as a tape which can be re-run.

Character repertoire. The total number of characters of each font × the number of different typefaces × the number of different sizes is the character repertoire. Linecasting machines use a single character matrix° for each typeface and size. A new magazine or matrix case is required for each change of face or type size. Phototypesetting machines have much greater character repertoires, ranging from a few thousand characters, to well over twenty thousand.

Less noise. Generally speaking, phototypesetting machines have fewer moving parts and are, therefore, much quieter than linecasters.

A cleaner method. The photographic process eliminates the use of hot metal (700°F) which is both a safety hazard and a cause of discomfort in warm weather or close quarters.

Corrections. The process of making corrections is clearly easier in slug composition (Linotype) than in phototypesetting. This seems to be the only major disadvantage of phototypesetting, although there are many acceptable cold-type correction techniques.

Manufacturers

There are hundreds of machine models available today, with more being introduced on a regular basis. The most up-to-date information can be received directly from the manufacturer for the price of a stamp.

Alphatype Corporation
7500 McCormack Boulevard
Skokie, Illinois 60076

Composition System Incorporated
570 Taxter Road
Elmsford, New York 10523

°*Linotype matrices usually have two duplexed characters, one a roman, the other an italic or bold.*

Compugraphic Corporation
80 Industrial Way
Wilmington, Massachusetts 01887

Graphic Systems Incorporated
217 Jackson Street
Lowell, Massachusetts 01852

Harris Corporation
Composition Systems Division
P.O. Box 2080
Melbourn, Florida 32901

ICS Sales and Leasing Incorporated
P.O. Box 281
313 North First Street
Ann Arbor, Michigan 48107

Information International
12435 West Olympic Boulevard
Los Angeles, California 90064

Mergenthaler Linotype Company
One Mergenthaler Drive
Plainview, New York 11083

MGD Graphic Systems
Rockwell International Corporation
2735 Curtiss Avenue
Downers Grove, Illinois 60515

The Singer Company
Singer Graphic Systems Division
151 Callan Avenue
San Leandro, California 94577

Star Graphic Systems Incorporated
240 South Main Street
South Hackensack, New Jersey 07606

SunCom Systems Division
Sun Chemical Corporation
575 Underhill Boulevard
Syosset, New York 11791

VariTyper Division
Addressograph-Multigraph Corporation
11 Mount Pleasant Avenue
East Hanover, New Jersey 07936

Phototypesetting Machines

An AM700 series phototypesetter.

The Mergenthaler V.I.P.

7 phototypesetting as a system

Summary

Phototypesetting is a *system*, a purposeful relationship of interacting devices. These devices, the people who operate them, and the material they produce, follow a production path or scheme called a *workflow*.

    This workflow begins with the generation of written or typewritten words which need to be converted to type. Before the *copy* reaches the hands of a keyboard operator, however, it must first be processed by an editor, an artist, a mark-up person and a department manager. Following conversion to machine coding by a keyboard operator, the output medium is proofed, corrected, and finally sent to the phototypesetter for the actual setting of type.

    The computer, which has made phototypesetting an economic reality, is actually a system itself. It has its own input and output, as well as sections to store, process, and control.

    Printing is the greater system into which phototypesetting fits. *Offset lithography*, the prevalent printing method, carries the typeset material through the entire process from mechanical art preparation to the finished printed product.

Trade Terms

binary number system - a number system written in base 2 notation.

bit - a *b*inary dig*it*.

byte - a consecutive series of binary digits.

copy - hand or typewritten material which must be converted to type.

copy writer - a person who writes copy. See copy.

core - ferrite rings used in computer memories to store binary information.

flat - an opaque sheet of paper or plastic onto which a lithographic negative has been taped. The negative is taped in exact position in relation to its ultimate appearance on the printed page. Windows are cut out of the carrier sheet to permit light to pass through the image areas for platemaking.

mechanical - a piece of prepared artwork and typography ready for camera. Derived from the reference to "mechanical art" as a synonym for "pasteup."

offset lithography - a major printing process based on the natural repellency of oil (ink) and water (fountain solution). The plate, wrapped around a turning cylinder and carrying a film of ink on its image areas, is brought in contact with a turning rubber blanket cylinder. Paper is fed between the blanket cylinder and an impression cylinder and the image is "offset" onto the paper.

peripheral - parts or devices external to a machine.

program (computer program) - a precisely defined set of instructions to direct the specific operation of a computer.

software - a computer term referring to programs and procedures rather than equipment (hardware).

stripping - the process of affixing negatives or positives onto a carrier sheet. The end product is a flat. See flat.

system - a group of parts, people and/or devices acting and reacting together to achieve an outcome related to the whole.

word - a series of bytes of a defined length.

workflow - the order in which parts of a system are processed.

Introduction

A system is a group of parts or devices which act and react together to achieve an outcome related to the whole. Phototypesetting is both a system in and of itself as well as a part of the greater system of printing.

A phototypesetting system, or any system for that matter, is not only concerned with the devices which comprise it, but also with the relationship of those parts to one another. The order in which parts fit together to perform the system objective is defined by the workflow. In a simple typesetting system, the workflow begins with the generation of copy, which must be converted to type. The copy is converted to machine readable codes recorded on an input medium. The input medium is used to drive a phototypesetting device producing galleys of photographic material suitable for reproduction.

System Components

The Copy. The phototypesetting production cycle begins when a need for typeset material is established. This need may take the form of an author's manuscript, a news story, an advertiser's message, a business report, or any number of other things. The copy is submitted to an editor.

The Editor. The editor checks the copy for style and grammar. He may specify the typefaces and line measures himself or may send the copy to an artist or designer.

The Artist. The artist considers the typographic design as well as the overall appearance of the finished printed piece. He forwards the copy to the mark-up person.

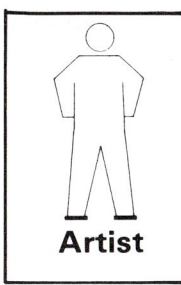
Artist

The Mark-up Person. The mark-up person translates the artist's specifications into machine codes. He delivers it to the typesetting department foreman or manager.

Mark-up Person

Foreman or Department Manager. The Supervisor of the typesetting department determines how (or if) the copy will be divided. The job may dictate that only certain machines be used due to a need for special typefaces or point sizes. He assigns either all or part of the copy to a keyboard operator.

Supervisor

The Keyboard Operator. The keyboard operator converts the copy into machine readable codes. The device used may be a counting or non-counting, blind or visual keyboard. The recorded input medium is then proofed.

Understanding Phototypesetting

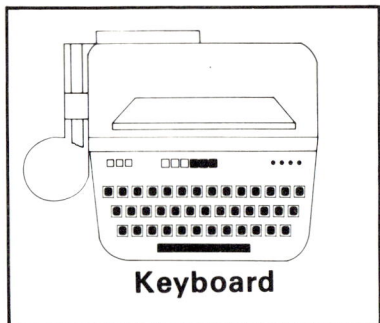
Keyboard

Proofing. The input medium may be proofed by running on the phototypesetter; by viewing on a VDT; by processing through a computer; by feeding through a matrix proofer; or, if produced on a special keyboard, by reading hard copy.

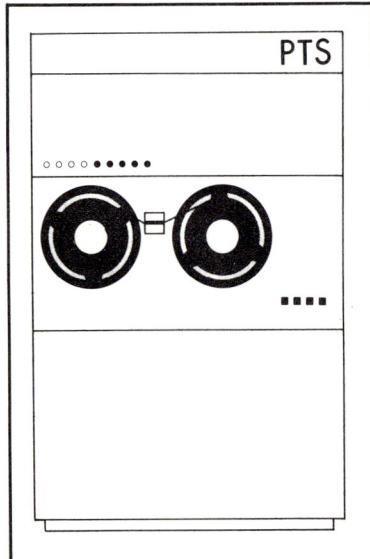

Phototypesetting as a System

Matrix Proofer

Dual Image Tape

Hard copy

Understanding Phototypesetting

The proof will be read and errors marked by the proofreader, and possibly by the author or customer.

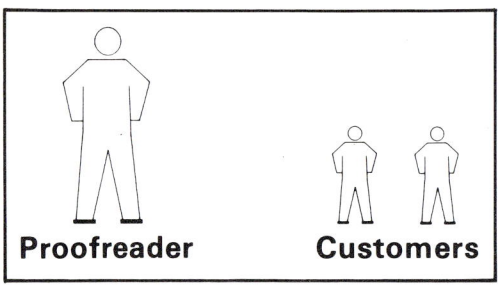

Correction. Errors found when using the phototypesetter as a proofer will be corrected by producing a correction input medium and either cutting or pasting the corrections into place on the galley or, by using a computer, merging the original input medium with the correction medium, or, if there are only a few easily found errors, by splicing corrections into the original input medium.

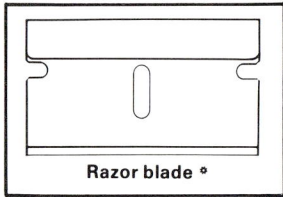
Razor blade °

Merging tape

Splicing tape

°*Razor blade should only be used in approved safety holders.*

Phototypesetting as a System

Errors found by using a VDT as a proofing device can be corrected at the time they are found by use of the editing keyboard.

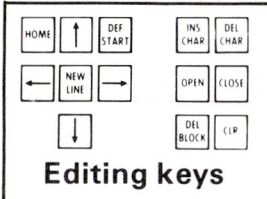
Editing keys

Errors detected on a computer or matrix proofer printout can be corrected by producing a correction medium keyed to the numbered lines containing errors, and merging it, by computer, with the original.

Errors found on dual image tape or hard copy would be reset and cut and pasted on the original galley.

Typesetting. The recording media used to drive a phototypesetter include perforated tape (6 or 8 channel), magnetic tape (reel, cassette, MT/ST, or IRT) punched cards, and OCR and dual image media.

Mag tape

Understanding Phototypesetting

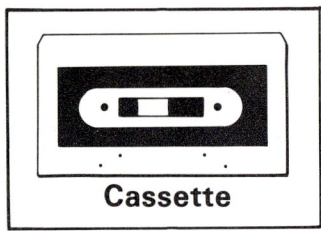
Cassette

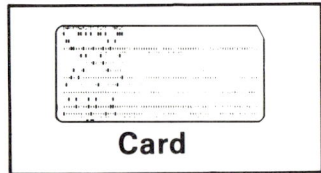
Card

Dual Image Tape

On-line devices which are wired directly to the phototypesetter and drive it by electrical impulses without the use of a direct recording medium include a computer, a VDT, and a direct entry keyboard.

Phototypesetting as a System

Direct entry keyboard

Output. The output of a phototypesetting machine is either a right or wrong (mirror image) reading photographic positive paper or film galley. The output requires chemical processing.

These components include most of the options available in phototypesetting systems with the present state of technology. The form taken by systems in use today is usually dependent upon the ultimate purpose and form of the work being produced as well as economic constraints, technological advances, and plant growth.

The Computer as a System

The first use of a digital computer in the typesetting area was in the early 1960s, when a general purpose computer, used for accounting and payroll functions, was programmed to hyphenate and justify perforated tape. Removing the end-of-line decision making from the perforator operator not only increased his speed, but also allowed him to produce a tape from a less sophisticated and less expensive keyboard.

One of the first computers built to perform a specific (special purpose) typesetting task was the Compugraphic *Linasec*. It was used to justify tape, but lacked the storage necessary for hyphenation, thereby requiring a monitor to respond to word breaks on a CRT screen. The Linasec was followed by the Compugraphic *Justape*, which had the ability to accept an unjustified tape and output a justified tape, without the aid of a human monitor.

Today, second and third generation phototypesetting machines have built-in special purpose mini-computers. These computers handle all of the H and J decisions as well as other typographic functions. Special application typesetting may require the use of additional, or peripheral computers, to perform such tasks as:

1. generating parts list
2. alphabetizing directories and indexes
3. listing current classified ads and deleting those which have expired
4. removing (stripping) end-of-line codes from wire service tapes to change the line measure, typeface, or point size.
5. paginating text
6. sorting and updating stored material
7. storing and retrieving news stores.

The computer itself is a system composed of five functional units. The input device is capable of sensing codes on a recording medium, such as perforated tape, and sending those codes to a storage area. The storage, or memory unit, holds input data as well as program instructions (what the computer is to do and how it is to do it) and the intermediate results of calculations. Data is moved from memory to the *arithmetic* unit by the *control* or central processing unit (CPU). The arithmetic unit is capable of performing basic calculations, comparisons, and tests at incredible speed. After the data has been processed, the control unit sends it back to storage where it is forwarded to an output device. The control unit directs all activities according to the specifications of the computer program. The program is an exact set of instructions and sequences which detail the exact operation of the computing process. Figure 1 shows a diagram of the major components of a computer.

Input codes are stored in memory on thousands of circular ferrite cores, which are capable of holding either a positive or negative magnetic polarity.

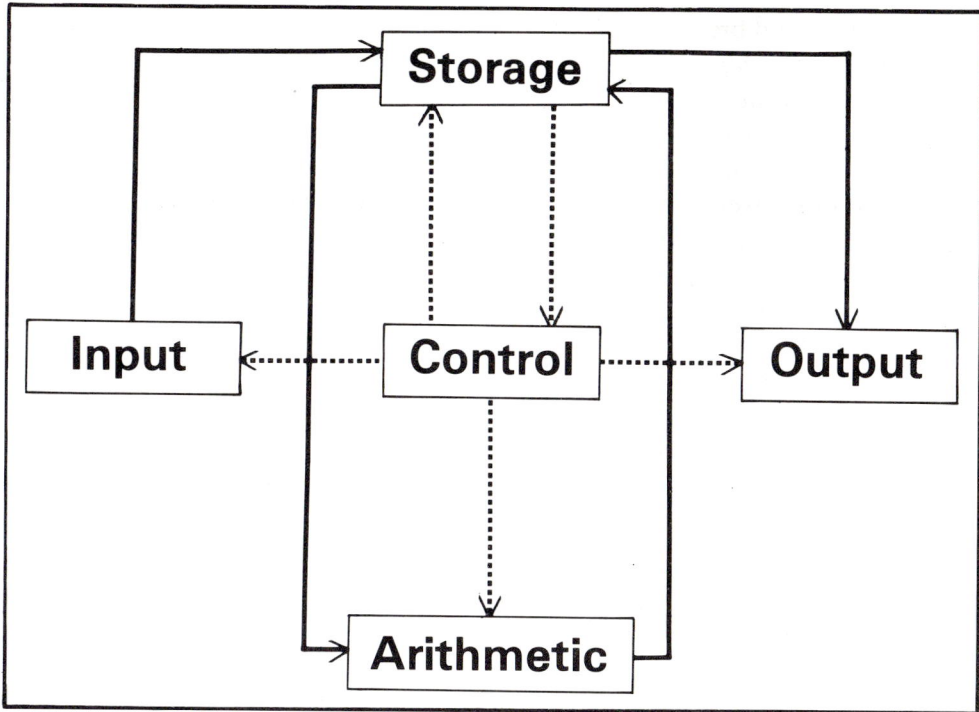

Figure 1. The major components of a computer.

A single core is called a bit for *binary digit*. Layers of core form words, which are made up of bytes. A byte is a sequence of adjacent bits which is considered an operating unit, just as a series of houses on a street would be considered a block. To review, bits (usually 8) make up bytes (usually 2) which make up words. The byte size and word size may vary from computer to computer. There is no standard measurement to compare computer storage capacities. Some computer manufacturers specify storage in terms of bytes, others use words.

The two magnetic states which a bit may take can be considered as representing either a "1" or a "0." The one and the zero are used in the binary number system to represent any decimal number. The binary system is based on the powers of the number two, as shown.

Power of 2	2^6	2^5	2^4	2^3	2^2	2^1	2^0
Decimal Value	64	32	16	8	4	2	1

Understanding Phototypesetting

Decimal numbers can be converted to binary by placing a one beneath each of the powers of two found in the number and zeros in the other positions, as shown.

Decimal Number	Binary Form						
	2^6	2^5	2^4	2^3	2^2	2^1	2^0
	64	32	16	8	4	2	1
1	0	0	0	0	0	0	1
2	0	0	0	0	0	1	0
3	0	0	0	0	0	1	1
4	0	0	0	0	1	0	0
5	0	0	0	0	1	0	1
10	0	0	0	1	0	1	0
100	1	1	0	0	1	0	0

The magnetic polarity, and therefore the binary status of a bit, is dependent upon a current which passes through two wires which cross through the center of the core ring.

One wire is labelled x, the other y. A third wire passes through the core in order to detect the direction of the magnetism. This "sensing wire" will carry the binary information to its next processing area.

Perforated and magnetic tape, punched cards and other recording media are capable of storing binary information for input into a computer. The punched holes in perforated tape, for example, activate selected bits, to cause polarity in one direction (giving a 1), whereas blanks cause the opposite polarity (giving a 0). The actual functioning of a computer is much more complex, yet this introduction should serve as a means of orienting the beginner.

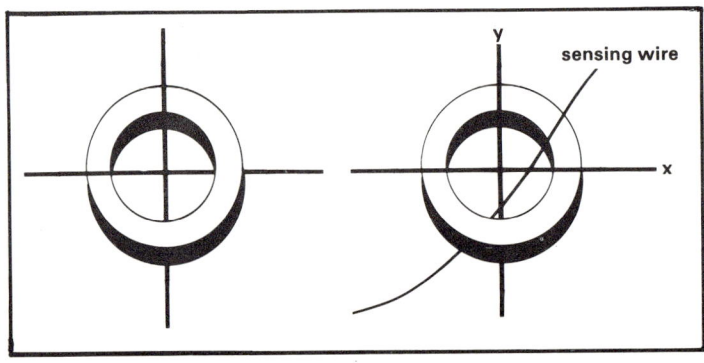

The Printing System

The ultimate use of almost all typesetting is for printing. Phototypesetting, in particular, meets the needs of offset lithography, a major printing process based on photographic and chemical principles.

The lithographic production cycle begins with the establishment of a need for a printed item. This need may take written form through the efforts of a copy writer or other person familiar with the message, or the need may have been previously established by either an author, in the form of a manuscript, or an advertiser, in the form of copy. In any event, drawings, illustrations, and the overall design are handled by an artist. Pictures are taken by a photographer. Type is specified (spec'ed) and set. The elements are all brought together and assembled in page format in a process called art and copy preparation.

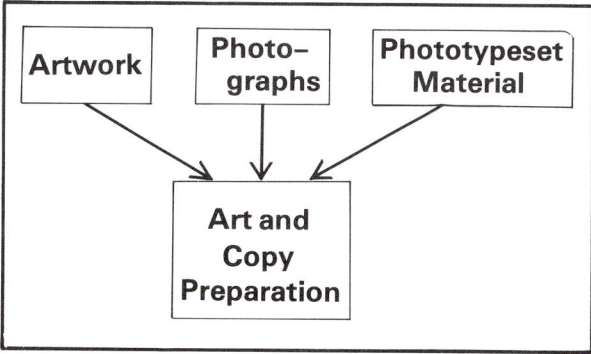

The artwork, photos, and type are "pasted up" in position to produce a mechanical, a completed page layout.

The mechanical is placed on the copyboard of a darkroom camera and photographed. The result is a photographic film negative.

Understanding Phototypesetting

The negative is "stripped" into position on a sheet of opaque orange (goldenrod) paper or plastic which is the exact size of the press plate. The negative, taped in position on the paper or plastic, is called a flat.

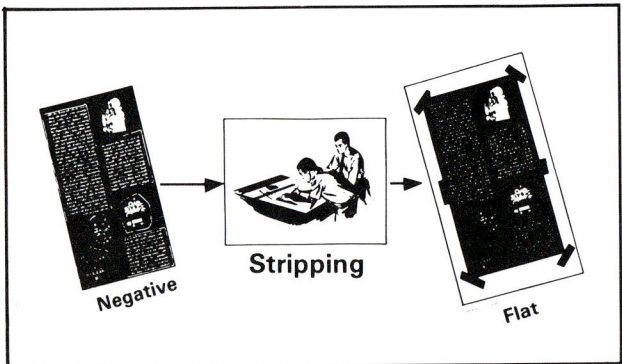

The flat is contacted, under vacuum pressure, to a flexible plate which has a light sensitive coating on its surface. The plate is exposed, through the flat, to an intense light source. The exposed plate is then chemically processed.

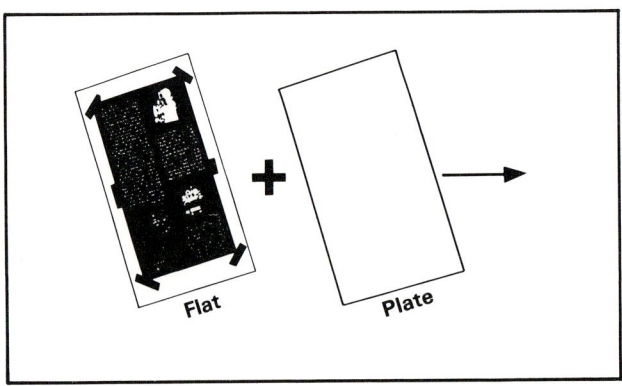

Phototypesetting as a System

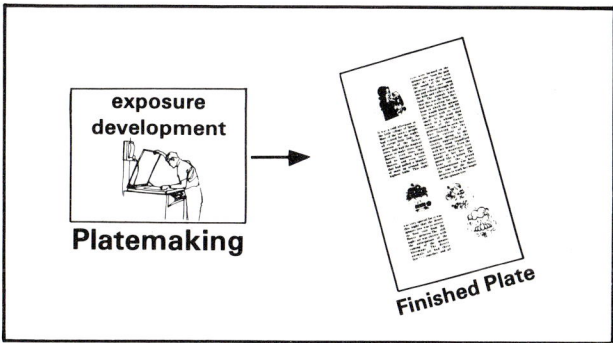

The finished plate is then mounted on an offset press plate cylinder. Chemically treated water keeps the non-image areas free of ink, while the image area attracts and holds ink. The plate cylinder turns against a rubber blanket cylinder onto which the image is "offset" or transferred. Paper passes between the blanket cylinder and an impression cylinder, "offsetting" the image onto paper.

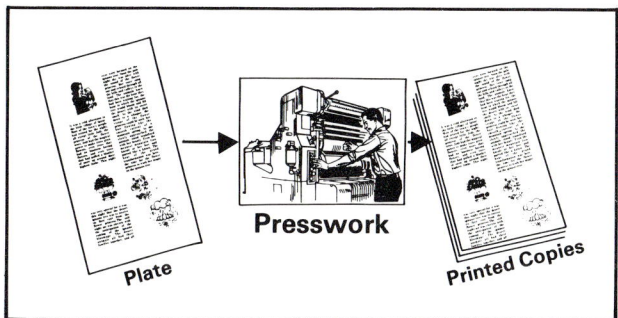

Although typesetting happens early in the printing cycle, it is carried through in every step along the way, and in a number of different forms (paste-up, film negative, flat, plate and printed page).

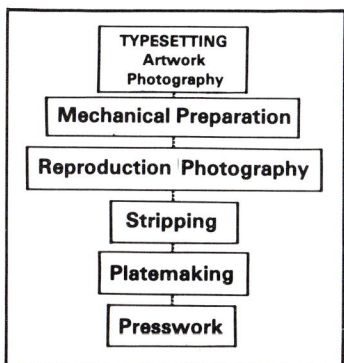

The Way it Was

Printing, being the end product of almost all typesetting, has various requirements dependent upon the process. The hot-metal typesetting system, prevalent since the late nineteenth century, produces a relief surface, and therefore serves the requirements of the letterpress printing process. Phototypesetting, on the other hand, produces a flat high-contrast image and is better suited to the requirements of offset lithography. The accompanying flow chart shows how a traditional hot-metal typesetting system functions.

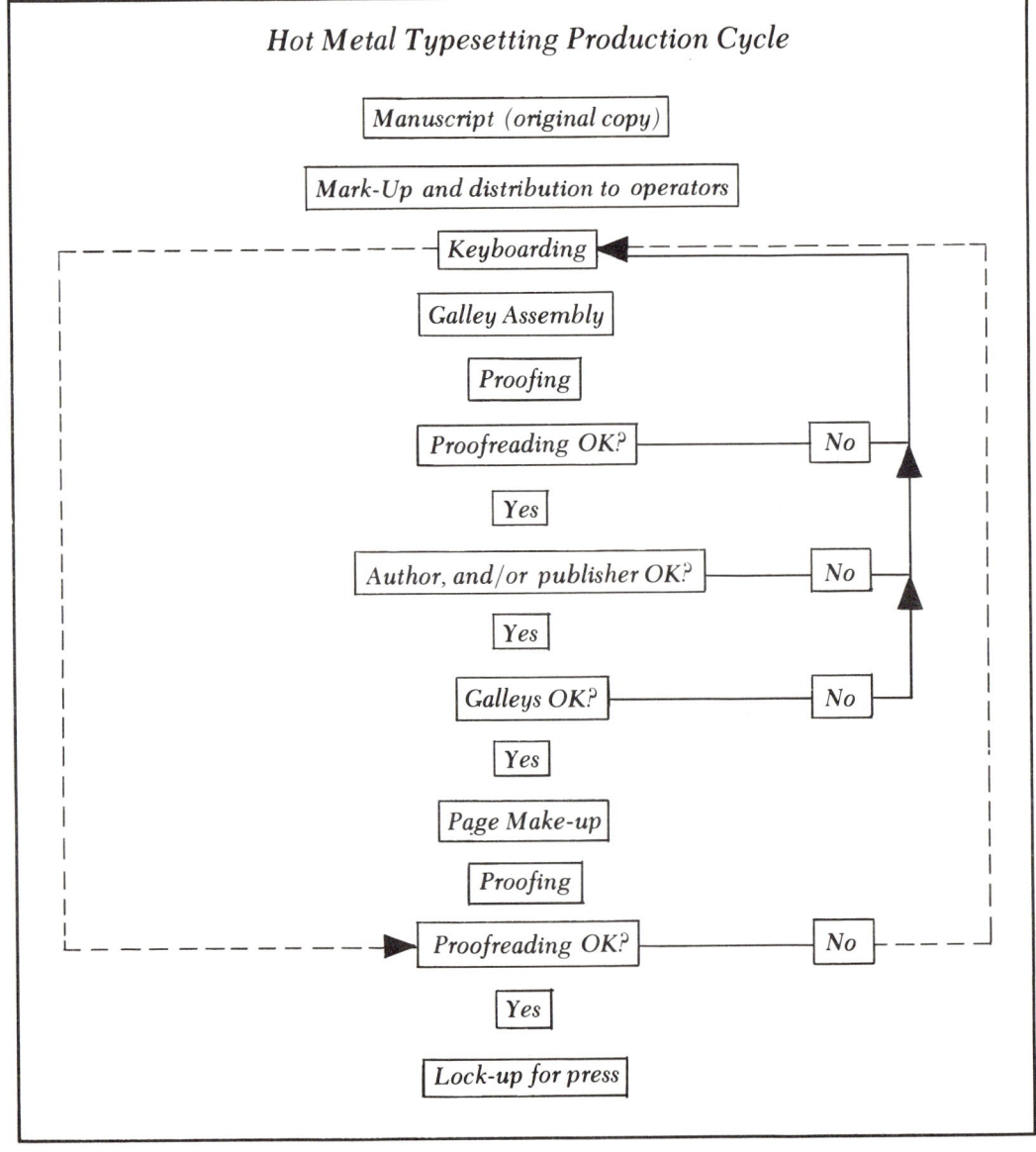

8 processing methods and materials

Summary

Exposed photographic materials have invisible or latent images which can be seen only after undergoing chemical processing. The image is formed in the *emulsion* layer of photographic film or paper by light striking crystals of silver halide. The silver halide becomes black during the developing stage forming a visible image. The material then undergoes an acid rinse to stop the developing activity and prepare it for the fixing solution. The *fixer* removes the unexposed silver halide crystals by making them water soluble. The material is then washed to remove all processing ehemicals, and then dried.

Stabilization papers have a developing agent manufactured in the emulsion. A special two solution processor is used to activate the developer and then immediately stabilize the non-image. This instant system eliminates a number of time consuming processing steps and makes it especially suitable for phototypesetting applications. Other light-sensitive materials used in phototypesetting machines include *RC paper*, positive film, and plate material.

Most light-sensitive materials exposed in phototypesetting machines are processed in *automatic processors*. Such machines save time and labor, and, depending upon the type of machine, also reduce chemical costs.

Trade Terms

antihalation - a dye used on the base side of film to prevent light from bouncing back to the emulsion.

base - the flexible support of a light-sensitive material.

development - the photographic processing step which changes exposed silver halide crystals to black metallic silver.

dimensional stability - the ability of a photographic material to maintain its size.

emulsion - the light-sensitive layer of photographic film and paper consisting of silver halide crystals suspended in gelatin.

fixer - sodium or ammonium thiosulfate which renders unexposed silver halide crystals water soluble.

latent image - an invisible image formed on a light-sensitive material during exposure. The image is made visible by processing.

negative - a photographic image carrier on a flexible transparent base in which the image area is clear and the non-image area is dense black.

orthochromatic - a light-sensitive coating or emulsion which is insensitive to red light but sensitive to the blue-green part of the visible spectrum.

overcoat - a protective layer of gelatin used to coat photographic films and papers.

photography - a word derived from the Greek, meaning "writing with light." The creation of images by a controlled exposure of light.

PMT - Photomechanical Transfer. A method of making reduced, enlarged, or same-size black-on-white reproductions without the use of a negative intermediary. (Kodak trademark)

RC paper - a photographic paper which has had its base coated with a resin during manufacture. Resin coated papers are more dimensionally stable, and more permanent than stabilization papers.

replenishment - the addition of fresh dosages of processing solutions to maintain the chemical strength of solutions in an automatic processor.

silver halide - the light-sensitive crystals in photographic emulsions.

stabilization processing - a two solution developing process which is quick but not permanent.

stabilization processor - a two solution machine which activates and stabilizes stabilization materials.

stop bath - a processing solution composed of acetic acid which neutralizes the developer and prepares the photographic material for the acidity of the fixer.

substratum - a supporting layer in a photographic paper or film which adheres the emulsion to the base.

tray processing - the manual processing of photographic materials by immersion and agitation in a number of trays, each holding a different processing solution.

Introduction

The output of a phototypesetting machine is an exposed light-sensitive material. The characters which have been flashed on its surface are *latent images*, that is, invisible recordings of light. In order to see the images, and render them permanent, it is necessary to subject the material to chemical processing. In order to understand how chemicals used in processing act on the photographic material, it is first necessary to understand how a light-sensitive material is constructed.

The Construction of Light-Sensitive Materials

Photographic film and paper are quite similar in their construction. Both have an overcoat or antistress layer of gelatin on their surfaces to protect the emulsion during processing. Directly beneath the overcoat, is the emulsion itself, the light-sensitive suspension of silver halide in gelatin. The emulsion is adhered to the base, the flexible support of the material, by a layer of substratum. These are the basic layers found in photographic papers. Photo-

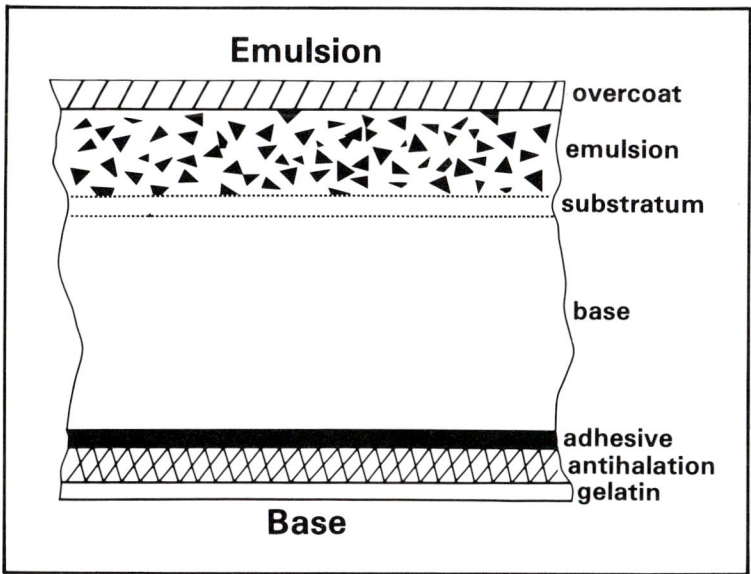

Figure 1. A cross section of the layers found in photographic materials. The bottom three layers are found only in film.

graphic films have three additional layers. The first is an adhesive layer which supports the second, an antihalation layer. This layer contains a special dye which absorbs light which passes through the emulsion, rahter than reflecting it back. A final layer of gelatin is coated on the base side of the film to prevent curling. A cross section of the layers found in light-sensitive materials is shown in Figure 1.

Exposure and Processing

The word photography is derived from two Greek words meaning "light" and "writing," or "writing with light." Light striking a light-sensitive surface precipitates a complex chain of reactions which ultimately result, through processing, in the conversion of silver halide crystals to metallic silver. The metallic silver appears dense black when developed, while areas not light struck appear clear. This high contrast black-on-white (paper), and black-on-clear (film), is characteristic of light-sensitive materials used in the graphic arts. Another characteristic of most light-sensitive materials used in graphic arts is their insensitivity to the red portion of the visible spectrum. This feature permits handling these materials, classified as orthochromatic, under red safe-light conditions.

Conventional photographic processing of black and white papers and films involves five major steps:

1. Developing
2. Rinsing
3. Fixing
4. Washing
5. Drying

These steps are involved regardless if the processing is by hand or by machine.

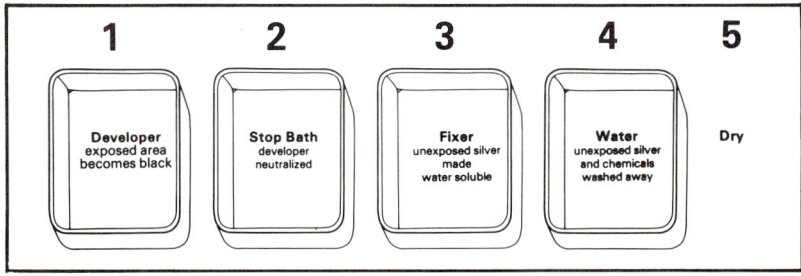

Figure 2. The steps involved in the conventional processing of black-and-white photographic materials.

The exposed photographic material is first placed in a developer solution, where the exposed grains of silver halide are acted upon. The developer reacts with the light-struck crystals to form minute irregular grains of black metallic silver. Development continues until the material is placed in an acid rinse or stop bath. The stop bath neutralizes the developer, which is still clinging to the material's surface, as well as prepares the material for the acid condition of the next solution. With development stopped, the material is placed in a fixing bath which removes undeveloped silver halide crystals from the emulsion by rendering them water soluble. The material is then washed to remove the chemicals of the fixing bath as well as the dissolved silver salts. Finally, the material is dried by either air (film) or contact to a heated surface (paper). The entire development process is shown in Figure 2.

Stabilization Processing

In 1961 two European manufacturers introduced a photographic paper which incorporates the developing agent into the emulsion. Its developing process not only eliminates the stop bath, washing, and drying steps, but also reduces the time needed to perform the remaining steps. Two processing solutions, an activator and a stabilizer, are used to form and fix the image. The activator is an alkaline solution which reacts with the incorporated developer to produce an image almost instantly. The stabilizer neutralizes the activator and changes any remaining silver halide crystals to relatively stable colorless compounds. Because the chemical activity has not been stopped, but only stabilized, the paper and the process is called stabilization. Stabilized images begin to fade in about six weeks and are very sensitive to strong light, high temperature, and excessive humidity.

The first stabilization papers required long or high intensity exposures. Only the strong light exposure of machines like the Fotosetter or Monophoto could be used. In March of 1966, Eastman Kodak introduced Ektamatic Grade S stabilization paper for use in lower intensity flash strobe phototypesetters.

Exposed stabilization paper is processed in a stabilization processor as shown in Figure 3. The paper travels through a roller transport and exits the machine in a few seconds, 80% dry and slightly tacky. The paper can be made permanent, if necessary, by use of the standard fix-wash-dry process.

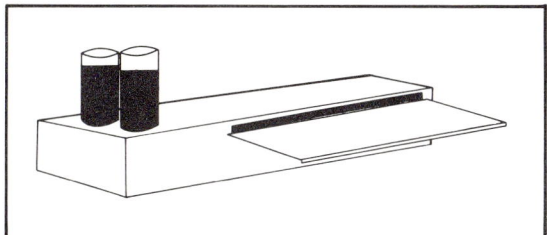

Figure 3. The stabilization processor uses two solutions to process typeset galleys for paste-up.

Other Light Sensitive Materials

RC paper. Stabilization papers are popular because they are quickly processed and inexpensively purchased. Yet, some phototypesetting applications require a paper with more permanence and less tendency to shrink and stretch. A coating or resin added to both sides of the paper base during manufacture greatly increases its dimensional stability, or ability to maintain its size. Resin Coated, or RC paper is also more permanent because it undergoes conventional processing, and is easier to paste up because it lies flat.

Film. Positive film captures the highest quality phototypesetting image due to its high degree of dimensional stability. It is widely used because assembled positive film images can be used directly for platemaking (positive working plates) rather than going to camera for a film negative. Presently, there is no easy way to get a film negative directly from a phototypesetter. Kodak, however, markets a Reversal Film Processor which will produce negatives directly from film positives, but it carries a $30,000 price tag.

Plate material. High speed lithographic paper plate material can be directly exposed in a phototypesetter using a xenon lamp or cathode ray tube. A special processor selling for about $14,000 is required. The plates' average press run is between five and six thousand impressions.

PMT.° Photomechanical Transfer (PMT) materials are commonly used to produce reproduction quality proofs from typeset galleys or paste-ups. The PMT process is a two step system for producing enlarged, reduced, or same-size reproductions from camera copy, without the use of a negative intermediate. First, copy is placed on a process camera copyboard and exposed to PMT negative paper, which is light sensitive. The exposed negative paper is sandwiched with a sheet of PMT receiver paper which is not light sensitive. Next, the two are fed into a diffusion-transfer processor which spreads activator between the papers and then squeezes them together. The actual processing takes from 4-1/2 to 6 seconds. After 30 seconds, the two sheets are peeled apart and the receiver paper is a finished reproduction proof suitable for a variety of uses.

Automatic Processors

Almost all output from phototypesetting machines is developed in automatic processing equipment. The simplest processor is the table-top stabilization processor which uses a constant drive speed and replaceable processing solutions. Larger automatic processors, used for film and RC paper, have variable speed motors to allow for photographic materials requiring different processing times. Another feature of large automatic processors is their ability to re-

---

°*Kodak trademark.*

use their processing solutions and maintain them at constant strength. They accomplish this by replenishing, adding fresh chemistry in measured doses to compensate for diminished solution strength due to processing.

Automatic processing, in general, is both time and labor saving when compared to tray (hand) processing. It also provides more consistent quality since the results are basically the same regardless of who is operating the machine, which is far from true in a tray processing situation. Finally, processors which use replenishment or recirculation of processing solutions greatly reduce the cost of processing chemicals.

The Pako Pakorol Super-G.

The Way It Was

The legitimacy of the offset lithographic process was recognized long before the general acceptance and use of phototypesetting, and its early practitioners were more or less dependent upon hot-metal typesetting to meet its requirements. In response to that need, a number of interesting products and machines were developed to convert the raised hot-metal image surface into a flat, high-contrast photographic one. Processes of this nature are collectively termed *conversion methods,* and although they are not of particular significance today, they do show an ingenious transitional period in typesetting.

The most prevalent and still-used conversion method is the *ink transfer* method. Using a reproduction proof press, most commonly the Vandercook, the metal typeform is inked with a fast-drying, dull black ink and is brought in contact with a sheet of high quality, coated reproduction paper which is rolled, under pressure, over its surface. The resulting reproduction proof is virtually camera-ready. A variation of this method involves the use of a paper, aluminum or zinc offset plate, instead of reproduction proofing paper, as an image carrier for direct use on an offset press or duplicator.

Another group of conversion processes are called *direct camera* methods because they photograph the metal typeform itself in order to produce a negative. One such method, the Brightype (see Figure 1), made by Ludlow Typograph Company, involves the spraying of metal typeforms with lampblack and the wiping and polishing of their surfaces. The resulting shiny metal surface is then illuminated with a circular bank of lights which surrounds the fixed-focus camera lens. Exposure and processing results in a negative. The method is expensive, messy (lampblack), time consuming, and most of all, like any conversion process which bypasses the reproduction camera, does not allow for enlargements or reductions.

A third conversion method, as typified by the *Instant Negative*, manufactured by Printing Arts Research Labs, involves the use of heat and pressure. A repro proof is pulled in the visual fashion using a special ink. It is then contacted with a ruby-colored film and heated in a vacuum frame for about a minute. The exposed film is processed under daylight conditions and the result is a negative.

Although many of these conversion systems are no longer in general use, they do present an interesting picture of the parallel between the development of typesetting and printing image carriers.

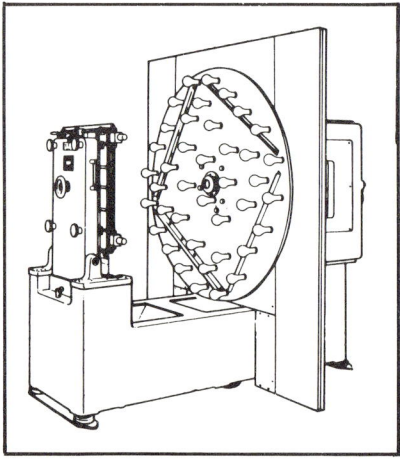

Figure 1. The Brightype, made by Ludlow Typograph Company.

9 paste-up methods and materials

Summary

Galleys of typeset material on paper and film are assembled by the processes of *paper paste-up* and *positive film make-up*. The assembly process positions type and other elements in the exact positions which they will take on the printed page.

    The *layout* is a carefully drawn sketch of how the paste-up or make-up will be executed. It includes all of the elements on a printed page (text, headlines, photos, and illustrations, etc.) as well as reference indicators.

    A number of adhesives are used to hold elements to their base supports. Among them are wax, rubber cement, adhesive tape, adhesive coating, adhesive spray, and double sided tape.

Trade Terms

ACM (Area Composition Machine) - a phototypesetter capable of setting any character or character group at the intersection of any x and y coordinates.

copy preparation - the mechanical assembly of type, illustrations, photographs, and artwork for photographic conversion.

doctor blade - a knife-edge blade pressed against the ductor roller of an adhesive waxer to control the thickness of wax.

fold marks - short marks printed in the margin of a printed piece to indicate folds.

grid system - a transparent plastic sheet carrying repeatedly used reference lines.

keying - coding parts of a manuscript with a letter or number designation in order to identify those parts to the compositor.

layout - a carefully drawn sketch approximating the appearance of the finished printed piece.

make-up - the assembly of film positives on a clear plastic base.

paste-up - the assembly of paper galleys on an illustration board or stable paper base for photomechanical reproduction.

register marks - a cross line design used in multicolor work to position colors subsequent to the first.

trim marks - short lines in the margins of printed pieces to indicate the finished size.

visual center - the center of a page as it appears to the eye rather than to the ruler.

workmarks - reference lines and marks used for positioning elements in a paste-up or make-up.

Introduction

Phototypesetters are generally used to output columns or blocks of type. Although machines do exist which are capable of complex advertising composition and tabular matter,° and full page composition and pagination, most phototypesetter output requires some cutting, pasting, and assembling, to position the type in the page location which it will ocupy when printed.

    The assemblage of text and display type, illustrations, and other artwork is generally termed copy preparation. Copy, positioned exactly as it is to appear when printed, is prepared for photographic conversion into a high con-

---

°*Such machines called ACM, Area Composition Machines, are able to set difficult display and text composition.*

Paste-up Methods and Materials

trast negative needed for offset platemaking. The reproduction camera is a sensitive instrument which will detect any imperfections in less than perfect copy.

Although much more than type is involved in copy preparation, this unit will cover only the assembling of paper galleys, called paper paste-up, and film galleys, called positive film make-up.

The Layout

The layout is a visual guide, or plan, for the exact positioning of elements on a page. Its purpose is to show in a drawing, how the finished printed piece will look (see Figure 1). It is usually drawn to size with headlines and subheads carefully penciled in, exact text area indicated and photographs and/or illustrations simply but clearly sketched. Exact instructions concerning typefaces, sizes, line lengths, color breaks, etc. are written in the margins, or on a tissue overlay, which also serves to protect the layout.

Figure 1. A layout is a guide showing where each element will be pasted in position.

Workmarks

The layout uses a number of reference lines and marks to orient each of its elements in a more discrete manner. Just as landmarks are used when giving travel directions to a lost driver, the reference points used on a layout are used as guides when making the camera-ready mechanical, and to some extent throughout the entire printing production cycle.

Reference lines and marks which will not be printed, but are used exclusively for partitioning off areas of the layout, are drawn in light blue non-reproducible pencil. They usually appear as broken lines. The first line drawn is usually the vertical center line.

The horizontal center line is equidistant between the top and bottom margins.

The mechanical center, however, usually appears to be below center. Artists, therefore, use a visual center line, a little above center.

Understanding Phototypesetting

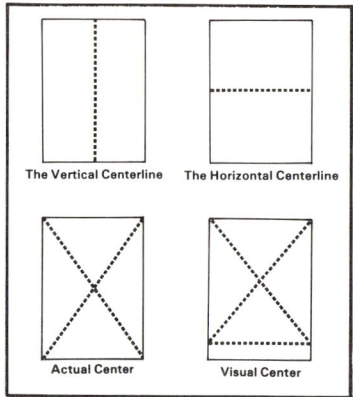

Trim marks, indicating where the printed sheet will be cut, are shown as fine short black lines in all four corners.

If the sheet is to fold, short black fold marks are shown in their proper places.

Multicolor work which will make more than one pass through a single color press, or through more than one unit of a multicolor press, uses register marks in the margins to correctly position subsequent colors.

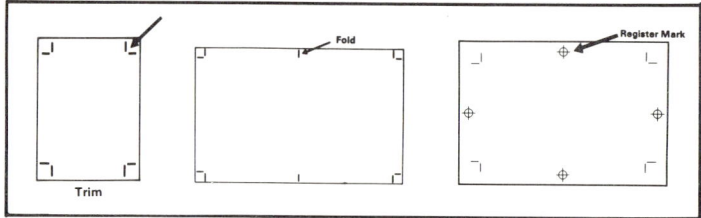

Reference lines of layouts which follow a standard arrangement, such as the style of a particular magazine or newspaper, are often drawn on acetate or mylar in light blue or black, and placed either over a sheet of paper as an overlay guide, or under, on a light table. Such a method, called a grid system saves the repetitive drawing of standard lines.

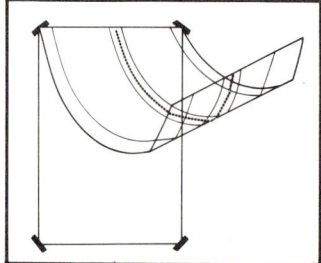

Paper Paste-up

Paper paste-up is the assemblage of layout elements which are carried on a photographic paper base. This method is used extensively in commercial and in-plant printing plants, as well as in newspapers. Using the layout as a guide, the paste-up elements are trimmed to within 1/16" to 3/8" of their image areas and then adhered to a rigid, smooth illustration board, or a translucent but stable paper.

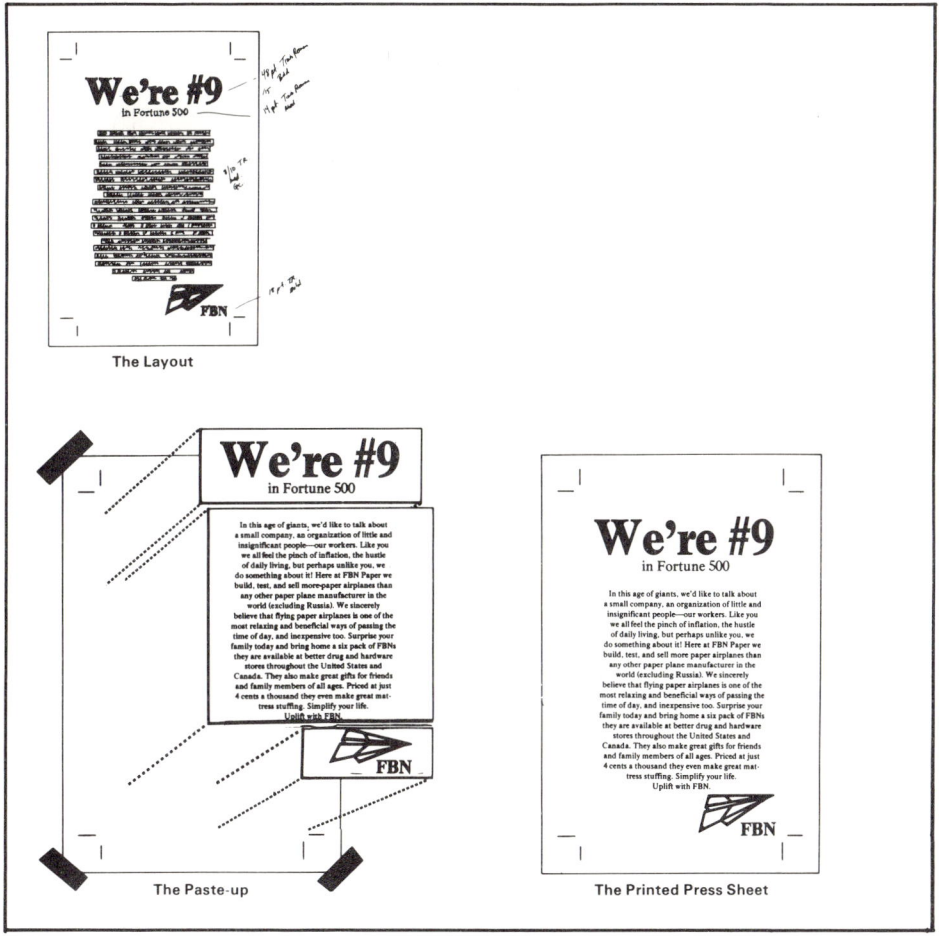

Paste-up Tools

Paste-up requires very close attention to detail since the reproduction camera will reproduce exactly what it sees. Typographical errors (typos), crooked lines, misplaced elements, fingerprints, dust, dirt, smudges, and any number of other problems should be located before the copy is photographed. The proper use of paste-up tools should eliminate any gross errors in alignment, measurement, or positioning.

The basic paste-up tools include:

A *T-square* to draw horizontal lines. It uses the edge of a drawing board or table as a vertical guide.

A *triangle* made of plastic or stainless steel is used with the T-square to draw vertical lines.

A *board*, or a *drafting* or *light table* is used as a work surface.

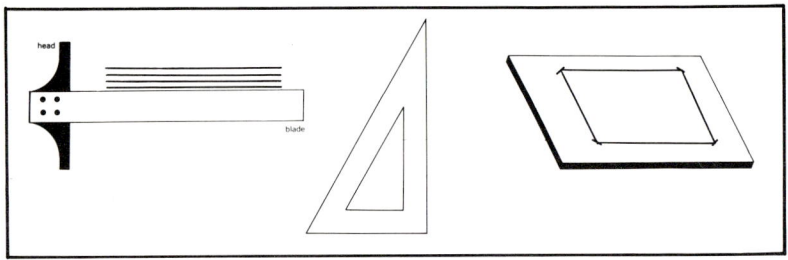

A sharp *pencil*, held at a 60 degree angle and rolled when used to evenly wear the lead and maintain a round point. Hard lead pencils, 2H - 4H are popularly used. A nonreproducible blue pencil is also necessary.

A *kneadable eraser* to remove extraneous pencil marks with minimal paper surface abrasion.

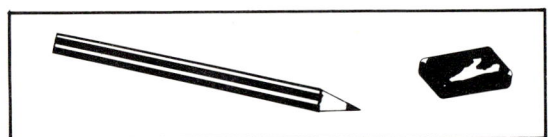

A *scissors* to cut layout elements to size.

A *knife holder* and *blade* or a *razor blade* and *holder* for precise trimming.

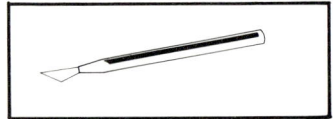

Paste-up Methods and Materials

A *ruling pen* to draw trim, fold, and register marks using *india ink*.

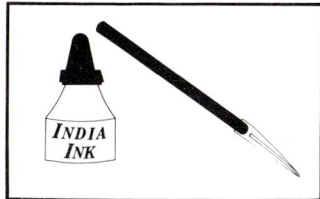

A white opaque *correction fluid* to paint over small unwanted image areas.

A *metal rule* calibrated in picas and inches for accurate measurements.

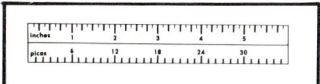

An inking or pencil *compass* for drawing circles.

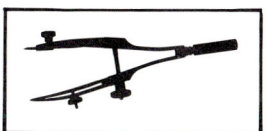

A *french curve* for drawing an irregular or curved line.

And finally, a red sable *brush* for touching up weak image areas with india ink.

Adhesives

There are a variety of ways in which elements in a paste-up can be adhered to a board or other base. The name "paste-up" itself is a good description of the process of cutting and gluing in position. Paste, however, is not commonly used today because of its consistency, texture, and moisture content. The criteria by which adhesives are evaluated include strength, coating thickness, and the ability to change position and retain tack.

Wax. Hot adhesive wax is applied by passing the paste-up material face up between the two turning rollers of a waxer. The bottom roller or ductor is situated in a thermostatically controlled pan of wax 140 - 190 degrees F. The top roller presses the material against the liquid hot wax surface of the ductor. The waxer, depending upon the model, applies either a solid or striped layer of wax evenly across the back of the material. The thickness of the layer is controlled by a doctor blade which removes excess wax from the ductor. The waxed element is then positioned, and burnished into place using roller or finger pressure.

A waxer, as shown in Figure 2, has the advantage of applying an even coat of temperature controlled wax which will retain its stickiness even if the paste-up element to which it is applied is removed and replaced. Wax which is applied at an excessive temperature, however, can penetrate paper and also lose its adhesive qualities.

Figure 2. An adhesive wax-coating machine lays a uniform coating of pressure-sensitive wax on a variety of materials.

Rubber cement. Rubber cement is a popular adhesive which does not wrinkle, curl, or shrink. It is stainless, flexible, and clear drying. Brushed onto a paste-up element, it is adhered while wet. It can be removed and repositioned at any time. A more permanent method of application requires coating both the element and the support surface and bringing them together after they have dried. Removing elements which have been permanently adhered may be accomplished by squeezing drops of stainless rubber cement thinner from a small oil can around the element, and lifting carefully.

Adhesive tape. Adhesive tape is not generally accepted as an effective means of mounting paste-up elements. Its shiny surface reflects when photographed, and its edges sometimes attract dirt. Double sided tape is sometimes used to adhere small paste-up pieces which are difficult to wax or rubber cement.

Adhesive coating. An adhesive coating machine similar in application to the waxer, but using a liquid adhesive, is another alternative. The system is generally more expensive than wax.

Pressure-sensitive adhesive spray. Adhesive spray from an aerosol can is an expensive but effective method of applying a sticky coating. This method is suggested only when expediency is of greater concern than cost.

Positive Film Make-up

Positive film make-up is basically the same as paper paste-up, except that film is substituted for paper, and a clear carrier sheet is substituted for illustration board or paper. Film gives a sharper character edge definition and also has superior dimensional stability. In addition, film make-up is generally more accurate and easier to accomplish since it can be assembled over a visible grid taped to the surface of a light table. It can be easily proofed using a diazo machine, or made into a litho negative by contacting. It can also be used as a transparent flat for making a positive-working plate.

Positive film galleys are trimmed and assembled on clear sheets of mylar, polyester, or acetate, with wax, static electricity, vacuum, stripping cement, or transparent or double sided tape. The tools used are the same as for paper paste-up.

Positive film make-up is the more expensive process in terms of materials; film is more expensive than paper. Yet, it is less expensive since it can bypass the camera stage altogether, and at the same time provide an image superior to paper paste-up. For these reasons, most trade typographers find this method advantageous.

See Bibliography for more extensive reading material.

BIBLIOGRAPHY

Anderson, P.L. "New Equipment Survey Shows...Why Phototypesetting Is Winning Out." *Printing Production* (December, 1969), pp. 43-48, 79-80.

———. "Taking a Fresh Look at Phototypesetters." *Newspaper Production* (January, 1973), pp. 53-6.

"'AP' Survey of Phototypesetting Equipment." *Australian Printer* (August, 1971), pp. 19, 21, 23, 25, 27, 29.

Auerbach on Automatic Photocomposition. Princeton: Auerbach Publishers, 1972.

Ballinger, Raymond A. *Layout and Graphic Design.* New York: Van Nostrand Reinhold Company, 1970.

Balzar, Friedrich. "Phototypesetting at the Drupa '72." *Newspaper Technology* (August, 1972), pp. 17-22.

———. "Quo Vadis OCR?" *Newspaper Society Production Journal* (July, 1972), p. 18.

Barrett, James J. "Keyboarding is More than Just Dexterity." *Newspaper Production* (November, 1972), pp. 42-44.

Boyd, Jim. "Phototypesetting: Correction and Editing Procedures." *Printing Equipment and Materials* (December, 1973), pp. 20-22.

"A Brief Review of Photosetter." *Printing World* (November, 1970), pp. 471-472.

Bruyninckx, Jozef. *Phototypography and Graphic Arts Dimension Control Photography.* Los Angeles: Ad Compositors, 1969.

Cabini, John F.J. *Copy Preparation for Printing.* New York: McGraw-Hill, 1973.

"The Changing Face of Printing. Part Two: Composition." *BFMP Members Circular* (February, 1973), pp. 48-50.

Cogoli, John E. *Photo Offset Fundamentals.* Bloomington, Illinois: McKnight Publishing Company, 1973, pp. 26-32.

———. *All You Need to Know About Photo Offset.* Philadelphia: North American Publishing Co., 1973.

"Copy Preparation." *Kodak Bulletin for the Graphic Arts* (November 22, 1970), pp. 1-9.

"Editing Devices: New Technology for Newsrooms." *Publisher's Auxiliary* (December 25, 1972), pp. 10-13.

"Equipment Survey." *Reproductions Review and Methods* (November, 1971), pp. 35, 37, 40.

Felten, Charles J. *Layout 4 Printing Design and Typography*. St. Petersburg, Florida: Charles J. Felten, 1970.

Gardner, Christina. "Copy Preparation Aids." *Business Graphics* (August, 1971), pp. 12, 14.

———. "Floating Images...and How to Pin Them Down." *Business Graphics* (January, 1974), p. 32.

———. "Waxing as a Paste-up Technique." *Business Graphics* (January, 1973), pp. 16, 18.

———. "Understanding Direct Keyboarding." *Business Graphics* (August, 1972), pp. 4, 6, 9-10.

———. *Effective Typesetting with the IBM Tape Composer*. Philadelphia: North American Publishing Co., 1973.

Graham, Walter B. *Complete Guide to Pasteup*. Philadelphia: North American Publishing Co., 1975.

Gray, Ben E. "Getting Started in Copy Preparation." *Reproductions Review* (February, 1971), p. 22.

Hartsuch, Paul J. "Small Computers for Medium-Sized Printers, Part I." *Graphic Arts Monthly* (July, 1973).

Higgason, Frank, "Markup for Phototypesetting". *Graphic Arts Monthly (November, 1972), p. 88.*

———. "Paste-up System and Equipment." *Graphic Arts Monthly* (October, 1972), p. 125.

———. "*Switching to Cold Type*." *Graphic Arts Monthly* (January, 1972), p. 66.

Hughes, Thomas. *Handbook of Operating Costs and Specifications for Phototypesetting Equipment*. Philadelphia: North American Publishing Co., 1975.

"In-Plant Printer's Directory of Typesetting Equipment." *In-Plant Printer* (February, 1972), pp. 20-22.

Jacobs, Marvin. *How to Establish a Cold Typesetting Department & Train Operating Personnel*. Philadelphia: North American Publishing Co., 1974.

Kamman, Alan B. "How to Pick CRT Terminals." *Data Processing Magazine* (April, 1971).

Karch, R. Randolf. *Graphic Arts Procedures*. Chicago: American Technical Society, 1972, pp. 71-129.

"Keyboard Equipment." *Publisher's Auxiliary* (December 25, 1972), pp. 13-14.

King, Howard. "What we've learned in 16 years of Photocomposing." *Printing Trades Journal* (December, 1969), pp. 33-35.

Lasday, Stanley B. *Handbook for Graphic Communications: Art and Copy Preparation, Composition, Conversion Processes*. Pittsburgh: Graphic Arts Technical Foundation, Inc., 1972.

Latimer, H.C. *Advertising Production Planning and Copy Preparation for Offset Printing.* New York: Art Directions Book Company, 1969.

Levy, William. "Copy Shape-Up." *Reproduction Methods* (February, 1971), pp. 17-20.

"1969—The Year That Was." *CIS Newsletter* (January, 1970), pp. 1-8.

Norton, Robert. "Display Photo-setting in the 70's." *Penrose Annual.* New York: Hastings House, 1972, pp. 179-189.

Olinghouse, Lane. "Changing Film on a Flat." *Modern Lithography* (June, 1973), pp. 25-27.

Orr, Kenneth, et al. *Printing Layout and Design.* Albany: Delmar Publications, Inc., 1968.

Outlook for Technology and Manpower in Printing and Publishing. Washington, D.C.: The U.S. Department of Labor, 1973.

Pakan, William A. "The Impact of Computerized Photocomposition on the Graphic Arts." *Visual Communication Journal* (1969-1970), pp. 30-33.

Palmer, Carl. "So You Want to be a Stripper." *Graphic Arts Monthly* (July, 1973), p. 77.

———. "Who Says the Computer Is Only for the Big Jobs? Photographic Procedure for Ad Production." *Graphic Arts Monthly* (April, 1973), p. 94.

Peter, John. "The Great Grid Controversy." *Folio* (January-February, 1974), pp. 31-38.

"Phototypesetting Equipment and Systems Part I." *Canadian Printer and Publisher* (October, 1972), pp. 39, 40, 45-49.

"Phototypesetting Equipment and Systems Part II." *Canadian Printer and Publisher* (November, 1972), pp. 29-38.

"Phototypesetting Equipment Currently Available." *Publisher's Auxiliary* (December 25, 1971), p. 4.

"Phototypesetting Input Equipment and Systems." *Printing Impressions* (July, 1975).

"Phototypesetting Output Equipment and Systems." *Printing Impressions* (June, 1975).

"Phototypesetting's Silent Majority." *CIS Newsletter* (February 1, 1971), pp. 1-2.

"Postscript to Photocomp Programs," *CIS Newsletter* (April 15, 1972), pp. 1-2.

"Recent Advances in Phototypecomposition." *Modern Technology* (April/May, 1970), pp. 9-13.

"Review of Typesetting Keyboards, Part I." *Graphic Arts Monthly* (March, 1973), p. 72.

"Review of Typesetting Keyboards, Part II." *Graphic Arts Monthly* (April, 1973), p. 76.

Riley, Wayne. "Pasting-up on Film" *Reproductions Review and Methods* (December, 1972), pp. 16, 20-21.

———. "Phototypesetting Today: Where Is It?" *Reproductions Review and Methods* (April, 1971), pp. 24, 52.

Rodgers, Vincent. "To Photoset or Not to Photoset." *Newspaper Society Production Journal* (July, 1972), pp, 5, 6, 9, 11, 12, 14, 16-17.

Romano, Frank J. "Choosing the Photocomposition Paper/Film/Chemicals You Need." *Inland Printer/American Lithographer* (February, 1973), p. 52.

———. *Handbook of Composition Input.* Mendota, Illinois: American Press, 1973.

———. "How to Get Started in Phototypesetting for Less than $20,000." *Inland Printer/American Lithographer* (October, 1972), p. 46.

———. "1984 is Here." *Book Production Industry* (December, 1972), pp. 21-22, 24-26.

———. "Pricing Photocomposition." *Inland Printer/American Lithographer* (November, 1972), p. 56.

———. "Today's Technology Shaping Tomorrow's Photocomposition." *Inland Printer/American Lithographer* (June, 1973), p. 44.

Salberg, Joel. "A Systems Approach to Photocomposition." *New England Printer and Lithographer* (October, 1970), pp. 35-38.

Sausele, George J.H. "25 Years of Phototypesetting Machine Research and Development." SPSE Symposium, October, 1972.

Silver, Gerald A. *Modern Graphic Arts Paste-Up.* Chicago: American Technical Society, 1966.

"Status Report: Typesetting Input Methods, Part I." *Graphic Arts Monthly* (August, 1972), p. 40.

"Status Report: Typesetting Input Methods, Part II." *Graphic Arts Monthly* (September, 1972), p. 78.

"Status Report: Typesetting Input Methods, Part III." *Graphic Arts Monthly* (October, 1972), p. 92.

Stevens, Mary E., and John L. Little. *Automatic Typographic-Quality Typesetting Techniques: A State-of-the-Art Review.* Washington, D.C.: Center for Computer Sciences and Technology, April, 1967.

Stevenson, Neil D. "The Design Elements." *The Australian Lithographer* (February, 1973), p. 21.

"Tools of the Trade." *American Press* (December, 1971), pp. 31-37.

"Typesetting Input Methods, Part III." *Graphic Arts Monthly* (October, 1972), pp. 92-93.

Van Wert, I. Gregg. "Phototypesetting . . . Trends and Developments." *Printing Magazine* (March, 1973), pp. 49-52.

———. "Poughkeepsie Daily Claims Mark-up System Major Factor in Phototypesetting." *Printing Magazine* (December, 1971), p. 38.

Wallis, L.W. "Phototypesetting Today, Part II." *Printing Equipment and Material* (December, 1972), pp. 10, 11, 13, 15.

———. "Phototypesetting Today, Part III." *Printing Equipment and Material* (January, 1973), pp. 10, 11, 13, 15, 16.

INDEX

a

AA's 85, 87
ACM 148
Activator 143
Adhesives 147, 157
Advanced feed (tape) 70
Agate line 1, 2
Alden typesetter 82
Alignment 59
Alphatype 112
Antihalation 140
Apex 2, 14
Arithmetic unit (computer) 132
Arm 2, 13
Artist 124, 135
Ascender 2, 6
Ascender line 17
ATF Spectype 43
ATF Typesetter 112

b

Backslant 22, 26
Bar 2, 13
Bar Codes 72
Base 140
Base alignment 17
Baseline 2, 17
Bawtree, A. E. 24, 25
Binary number system 123, 133
Bit 59, 71, 123, 133
Blackletter 18
Blair, J. C. 48

Blind keyboard 58, 59, 64, 88, 125
Blind (machine) 21, 22, 28, 30
Boldface 1, 2, 16
Border 20
Bouncing 21, 22, 25
Brightype 146
Buffer 40
Byte 123, 133

c

CAM 85, 95
Cap line 2, 17
Caption 20
Capturing Keystrokes 72
Card Comp 71
Cassette 22, 29
Cassette, magnetic 71, 129, 130
Caster, Monotype 5
  See also Monotype.
Center alignment 17
Center feed (tape) 70
Centering, direct impression 51
Central processing unit (cpu) 132
Central Type Foundry 48
CG 7200 39–41
Channel, tape 67
Character compensation 12
Character count 2, 8
Character repertoire 101, 119
Characters 2
Character set 95, 101
Character size 95
Chartpak 43

Church, Dr. William   61–62
Clean tape   85
Cold-type composition   47
Columns   20
Composing stick   12
Composition   2, 5
    capital   16
    lower case   16
Comp/set 500   74–75
Compugraphic Videosetter   114
Compugraphic Videosetter grid   114
CompuSystems   71
Computer   122, 126, 129–30
Computer card   71
Computer, editing   88–89
Computer system   131–34
CompuWriter   64
CompuWriter Jr.   75, 106
Condensed   22, 26
Conversion methods   146
Contact (exposure)   21–23, 30
Control case shift   68
Controller   85
Copy   122–24
Copyfitting   2, 8, 80
Copy preparation   135, 148–49
Copy reading   85–86
Copytype   36–37
Copy writer   123, 135
Core   123, 132–34
CorRecTerm   89–90, 93
Correction methods   128
Cost of phototypesetting   118
Counting keyboard   58–59, 63, 125
Crossfield CRT   114
CRT display   59, 65, 74, 84, 89, 132
CRT typesetters   100, 101, 112–115, 117
C-Thru lettering   43
Cursive   2, 19
Cursor   85, 91, 95
Cursor controls   92–93
Curving   21–22, 27

d

Datatype   72
Data window   91

Daylight operating   22
Delta Data Systems Corp.   90
Descender   2, 6
Descender line   17
Developer cell   34
Development   140, 142–43
Dictionary look-up   101
Diffusion-transfer processor   144
Digi-Data Corp.   72
Digiset   112–13
Digital storage   101
Dimensional stability   140, 144
Direct camera   146
Direct entry   59, 61, 63, 74
Direct entry keyboard   130
Direct entry typesetting   47
Direct image typesetting.
    See Direct impression typesetting.
Direct impression typesetting   46–57
Disc   100, 101, 105
Discretionary hyphen   59, 67, 117
Display   22
Display type   2, 21, 23
Distortion lenses   26, 44
Doctor blade   148, 157
Double keyboarding   89
Drum   100, 101, 105
Dual image tape   129–30
Duplicator   146

e

Ear   2, 14
Editing   84–85
Editing devices   84–99
Editing functions   95
Editor   124
Ektamatic processor   143
Elite   47, 52
Em   1, 2, 7–8
Emulsion   139–41
En   2, 8
End-of-line decision   59, 63, 131
End-of-line information   116
Escapement   47, 52, 54
Exception dictionary   101, 107
ExecuWriter Display   39–40
Expanded   22, 26

f

Face value 59, 76–78
Fairchild PhotoTextSetter 2000 112
Fanfold 59
Film advance 12, 76–77, 101, 104, 116
Film, positive 144
Film strip 100, 101, 106–8
Filmotype 28–29, 34, 37
First generation 100–2, 110
Fixed space 11, 47
Fixed space (typewriter) 52
Fixer 139–40, 142–43
Flat 123, 136
Floating display 59, 65
Fold marks 148, 151
Folio 20
Font 1, 2, 14–15, 68
Foreman, typesetting 125
Format 59, 66
Format, VDT 95
Formatt 43
Fotosetter 110–11, 143
Foundry type 2
Frame, tape 67
Friden Justowriter 56
Friese-Greene, W. 25

g

Galley 101, 117, 124, 128–29, 131, 143–44, 147, 149
Gelatin 141
Glidden, Carlos 48
Goldenrod 136
Graphic Developments Inc. 44–45
Graphic Systems I 76
Grid, font 100, 101, 108, 114
Grid system 148, 152
Gutter, page 20

h

Hand composition 2, 10, 12, 83
H and J 64, 116, 131–32
Hard copy 59, 64, 126
Hardware 59
Hard wire 59, 63
Harris Fototronic CRT 114
Harris Fototronic disc array 105
Harris 2200 95
Harris TxT UJ Perforator 65–66
Headline 3, 15, 20
Headliner, AM 31–33
Headliner, parts 33
Heden, S. J. 9
Hell Digiset 114
Higonnet, R. 112
Horizontal spacing 47
Hot metal 3, 5
Hot metal typesetting 145
Hot zone 59, 63
Hyphenation 116–17
Hyphenless justification 59, 64, 116

i

IBM Electronic Selectric Composer 56
IBM Executive 56
IBM MT/ST 72–73, 129
IBM Selectric Composer 46, 48–53, 55–57
Illustration 19
Image master 101, 105
Impact typesetting. *See* Direct impression typesetting.
Increment 101
Indention 11
Ink transfer 146
Input 59, 61
Input device, computer 132
Input devices 58–83
Input medium 124
Input options 118
Input/output 73
Input Revision Typewriter 59, 73, 129
Instant Negative 146
Instantype 43
Interface 60, 71
Interlock 60
Intertype Fototronic 112
Intertype Fototronic 1200 112
Italic 1, 3, 16, 18, 22, 26
ITCA 61

j

Justape 132
Justification 1, 3, 11, 116–17
Justification, direct impression 51, 54
Justified tape 60
Justowriter.
    See Friden Justowriter.

k

Kameratype 42–43
Kerning 3, 11, 27
Keyboard 3, 58, 61
Keyboard, blind.
    See Blind keyboard.
Keyboard layout 1, 3, 10, 60, 73–74
Keyboard operator 125
Keyboard operator (Monotype) 5
Keyboard (photolettering machine) 21–22,
Keying 148

l

Lanston, Tolbert 88
Laser 101, 114
Laterally reversed 22, 42
Layout 3, 147–49
Layout, keyboard.
    See Keyboard layout.
Leads 12
Leading 1, 3, 12, 76, 78, 104, 116
Legibility 3, 20
Letraset 43
Letterspacing 1, 3, 11
Letterspacing, direct impression 51
Light-sensitive materials, construction 141
Linasec 131
Line length 13, 115
Line length, direct impression 50
Line printer 89
Line spacing.
    See Film advance.
Linofilm 112
Linofilm Quick 112
Linofilm Super Quick 112

Linotron 303 114
Linotron 505 114
Linotron 1010 114
Linotype 3, 5, 10, 25, 46, 56, 61–62, 82–83, 110
Lithography 25, 110, 115, 122
    See also Offset lithography.
Logic program (hyphenation) 117
Lower magazine 106–7
Lower rail 107
Ludlow 23
Ludlow Typograph Company 146

m

Magazine 3, 5
Magazine, Intertype 107
Magnetic 71
Mainstroke, character 9
Make-up.
    See Positive film make-up.
Manufacturers, phototypesetters 119–20
Manufacturers, VDT 98–99
Mark-up 58, 60, 76–80
Mark-up person 125
Matrices 5
Matrix Electrostatic Writing Technique (MEWT) 96
Matrix proofer 85, 96, 126, 129
Mean line 3, 17
Measure 3, 8, 115
Mechanical 123, 135, 150
Media carriage 102
Mergenthaler VIP 106, 109, 121
Merging 128–29
Metric type size 9
Mill, Henry 48
Mini-computer 132
Mixing 3, 22, 27, 60
Mnemonic 60, 68–69, 76
Modern (typeface) 18
Monophoto 111, 143
Monospace 85, 91
Monotype 3, 5–6, 10, 25, 46, 56, 61, 63, 83, 88, 110
Morey, Walter 62
Moyroud, L. 112
MT/ST.
    See IBM MT/ST.
Mylar 60

n

Negative, film 135, 140
Non-counting keyboard 58, 60, 64, 88, 125
Nut.
    See En.

o

OCR 10, 60, 72–73, 84, 129
Off-line 58, 60, 63
Offset lithography 123, 135, 138
    See also Lithography.
Offset press 146
Old English.
    See Blackletter.
On-line devices 130
Orphan 3
Orthochromatic 140, 142
Output 60, 131
Output, computer 132
Overcoat 140–41
Overlap 22, 27
Overset 60

p

Page, parts 19
Paper tape, technical information 70
Parallel justification 47, 55
Paste-up 147–48, 152
PC board 63
Perforated tape 129
Perforating keyboards 88
Perforator 58, 60, 67
Peripheral 123
Photocomposition 102
Photographic processing, conventional 142
Photography 140, 142
Photolettering 21–45, 102
Photon 200 112
Photon 713 112
Photon Zip 112
Phototypesetting 3, 5
Proportional width.
    See Set width.

Phototypesetting, defined 102
Phototypesetting machines 100–21
Phototypositor 26, 34–35, 37
Pi characters 115
Pi font 22, 41
Pica 1, 3, 8
Pica (escapement) 47, 52
Plate material 139, 144
Platen, typewriter 47
PMT 140, 144
Point 1, 3, 8
Point size 4, 109
Point size range 115
Positive film 139
Positive film make-up 147–48, 158
Precedence code 60, 68–69
Prestype 43
Primary dimension 9
Printing system 135–37
Processor, automatic 139, 144–45
Program, computer 123
Projection (exposure) 21–23, 34
Proofing 126
Proofreader's marks 4, 86
Proofreading 84–86, 128
Proofs 85
Proportional spacing 46–47, 52
Prozsolt, Eugen 23
Punched cards 71

q

Quad 4
Quad left, direct impression 51
Quad right, direct impression 51
Quadding 4, 11

r

Race II system 71
Ragged right 4, 11
RC paper 139–40, 144
RCA Videocomp 112
Readability 4, 13, 20
Recording medium 60
Redactron 73
Red ribbon shift 68

Register marks   148, 151
Relative unit   4, 7, 11
Remington, E.   48
Replenishment   140, 145
Reversal film processor   144
Reverse leading   102
Reverse tape feed   66
Right reading   2
Roman   4, 18
Rub out   60, 66
Rubber cement   157–58
Rule   47, 51–52
Running tape   60

S

Safelight   142
Sans serif   4, 19
Script   19
Second generation   100, 102–3, 105, 112
Screen capacity   94
Screening   21–22, 27
Scrolling   85, 90–91
Secondary dimension   9
Secretarial shift   60, 66
Serial justification   47, 55
Serif   1, 4, 18
Set solid   4, 12
Set width   4, 6–7
Shadowing   21–22, 27
Sholes, C. Latham   48
Silver halide   139–42
Singer 9400   91–92, 94
Singer Photo Display 70   40–41
Singer Photomix 8400   76
Size range   102, 118
Slug   4–5
Small caps   1, 16
Software   123
Soule, Samuel W.   48
Space out   46–47, 54
Spec (type)   135
Speed, phototypesetting machine   117–18
Splice   60
Splicing tape   88, 128
Sprocket   60, 67
Spur   14
Square serif   18
Stabilization paper   139, 143–44

Stabilization processing   140, 143
Stabilization processor   140, 143–44
Stabilizer   143
Stack   22, 28
Staggering   21, 23, 26
Staromat   37–38
Stem   4, 13
Step and repeat   23, 27
Stop   67
Stop bath   140, 142–43
Stop bath cells   34
Storage computer   132
Strike-on.
    See Direct impression typesetting.
Strip   61
StripPrinter   30
Stripping   123, 136
Stripping (tapes)   132
Subhead   4, 20
Substratum   140–41
Super shift   61, 66, 68
System, phototypesetting   122–23

t

Tail   14
Take   61
Tape, adhesive   158
Teletypesetter System   62–63, 67
Third generation   100, 102–3, 112
Tick mark   102, 105
Tools, paste-up   154
Transfer type   43
Transposition   85
Tray processing   141, 145
Trim marks   148, 151
TTS code   61, 67–69, 71
TTS shift   61
Turret, font   100, 102, 108
Turret, lens   101, 109
Type   1
Type body   6
Type element   47
Type size   4, 16
Type size, direct impression   50
Type size, metric   9
Typeface, decorative   19
Typeface design   15

Typefaces, direct impression   49–50
Typeface geometry   17
Typeface, variations   1
Typemaster   31
Typewriter   47
Typesetting system, hot metal   138
Typography   1, 5
Typo   154
Typographer   4, 10
Typography   4–5
Text (size)   4, 8, 15, 23

U

Unjustified tape   61
Upper magazine   106–7
Upper rail   107

V

Vandercook   146
Variable space   11
Varigraph   41–42
VariTyper   46, 48–53, 55–57
VariTyper Electro/set 450   91–92
VDT   126, 129–30
Varsatec Corp.   96–97
Verso   20
Vertex   4, 14
Vertical spacing   47
Video typewriter   91
Visual center   148, 150

Visual display   58, 61, 64
Visual Display Terminal   84–85, 89
Visual keyboard   125
Visual (machine)   21, 23, 34

W

Warde, Beatrice   13
Warlock Computer Corp.   71
Wax, adhesive   157
Waxer, adhesive   157
Width plug   61, 63–64
Widow   4
Wooden blocks   81
Word   123, 133
Word processing   61, 72–73
Wordspacing   1, 4, 11–12
Workflow   122–24
Workmarks   148, 150
Wraparound   95
Write head   71

X

X-height   4
Xenon   103

Z

Zoom lens   102, 109